HEADWAY

TEACHER'S BOOK   ADVANCED

John & Liz Soars

Oxford University Press

Oxford University Press
Walton Street, Oxford OX2 6DP

Oxford New York Toronto Madrid
Delhi Bombay Calcutta Madras Karachi
Kuala Lumpur Singapore Hong Kong Tokyo
Nairobi Dar es Salaam Cape Town
Melbourne Auckland

and associated companies in
Berlin Ibadan

Oxford and Oxford English are trade marks of
Oxford University Press

ISBN 0 19 433565 8

© Oxford University Press 1989

First published 1989
Sixth impression 1993

Set by Promenade Graphics Limited,
Cheltenham, England

Printed in Hong Kong

Acknowledgements
The publishers and authors would like to thank
the following for their kind permission to use
articles, extracts, or adaptations from copyright
material:

Helen Franks: 'I Wanna Hold Your Hand' from
the *Guardian* of 4 December 1979.

The Rt Hon W W Hamilton MP: 'An Open
Letter to Her Majesty Queen Elizabeth II' from
My Queen and I.

Pan Books Ltd: extract from *What the Papers
Say and How They Say It* by Fritz Spiegl.

Introduction

Description of the course

Headway Advanced is the third volume of a comprehensive course for students learning English in their own countries and in the United Kingdom.

The aims of the course are to encourage students to analyse the systems of language in use, to expose them to a variety of challenging and interesting text-types in the listening and reading activities, and to stimulate them to give their own opinions and participate in discussions and roleplays.

Headway is a revision and extension course which provides a comprehensive coverage of the grammatical and lexical systems of English, combined with extensive practice of the four language skills. *Headway Advanced* can be used, with some supplementary examination-type exercises, to prepare students for the Cambridge Proficiency examination.

It provides approximately 120 hours' work, that is, ten hours per unit plus approximately four hours for the orientation unit. This has to remain a somewhat artificial calculation, as teachers can expand activities or cut them short to meet the needs of their students and their timetable. The Workbook is an important component, and it contains not only further practice of the language areas dealt with in the Student's Book, but also extra related input.

Key-notes

A course book for the advanced student

It is only recently that course books have been written for the advanced student. There were supplementary books to provide practice in the four skills, and grammar practice books, but it was somehow considered that an advanced class was too disparate, and the advanced student's needs too specific, to be catered for by one book. This is not necessarily any more true of the advanced level than any other level. There is perhaps the feeling that what unites a class below advanced is the collective need to 'climb the structural ladder', but the advanced student has 'done' all the structures, so it would be inappropriate to have a course book which prescribes the language areas covered. Students have undoubtedly been introduced to many aspects of the language, and have had considerable exposure to English, but there are still gaps in their knowledge, and it is possible to devise a broad-based syllabus consisting of revision and new input of both grammar and lexis. Added to this, there is a strong reassuring feeling for a student who can say, 'This is my English course book; I know what it's doing; I can learn from this,' and there is no reason why this should not also be true for the advanced student.

There is usually a degree of frustration for advanced level students. Whereas at low levels, progress is rapid and visible, at the advanced level the opposite is the case. Advanced students need to have the knowledge they possess confirmed via all kinds of productive and receptive activities and revision exercises, so that they get a certain boost of confidence. Reading extracts from literature and the quality press, listening to unscripted interviews with well-known (and not so well-known) English and American characters, and discussing contemporary issues should help students to realize that reaching an advanced level in a foreign language represents a considerable achievement. They need to be stimulated and challenged by a wide variety of material, so that they want to be involved, and so that their interest in the task does not wane. Their production of English, both spoken and written, needs to be diagnosed for error, so that areas of weakness can be pinpointed and worked on. Language items that perennially cause problems need to be revised. They also need to be expanded on by further study, because at lower levels it is often thought wise not to present students with all the information about an item, as it might confuse them and have little immediate utility value. At the advanced level, however, language analysis can be profound and comprehensive. Finally, there needs to be a significant amount of lexical input, so that students can express themselves with precision, and with a good command of idiom and collocation. *Headway Advanced* aims to work on these areas.

A course book for the teacher of advanced classes

Many teachers, both native-English speakers and non-native, fight shy of taking advanced classes. They feel that their own knowledge of the grammar is inadequate to deal with students' questions, or that the students will know more than they do. These are both realistic considerations, and nothing probably makes a teacher feel more confident than a profound knowledge of the language. In *Headway Advanced*, the Grammar section at the back of the Student's Book provides essential rules of form and use, and compares and contrasts items which are easily confused. In addition, there are notes on the language input in each unit of this Teacher's Book, which give the teacher further information, and where appropriate, examine an area in greater depth. There is also a great deal of explanation and provision of background information in the Teacher's Book. Answers to exercises and comprehension questions are given, naturally, and also an explanation as to why *x* is the answer if this is not totally apparent. If students are asked to write questions about an author or a British institution, then there are notes in the Teacher's Book to help you.

Another important ingredient of successful advanced teaching is having intrinsically interesting material that students would want to interact with in their own language. This should provide a basic motivation that pervades the whole course. We have selected a wide variety of material on a wide variety of topics, from sources such as nineteenth and twentieth century literature, quality newspapers and magazines, autobiographies, reference books, and interviews with personalities and experts in their own fields.

Another 'fear' of advanced teachers is that they will run out of material. Advanced students can get through material at an alarming rate, leaving the teacher wondering what to do next. The Workbook contains many exercises, both closely and loosely connected with the Student's Book. It has further gap-fill reading passages, and its own syllabus for pronunciation, multi-word verbs, idioms, and preposition collocations. Furthermore, in each unit of the Teacher's Book, there is an Extra Ideas section, which gives suggestions for incorporating issues and material that are current at the time the teacher is using the unit.

Finally, just as students benefit from having a course book, so teachers should feel reassured by having a framework and a direction on which they can build. It can be difficult to make a series of lessons cohere at this level. The topics and language areas dealt with in *Headway Advanced* should form a firm foundation for the course.

The organization of the course

Headway Advanced begins with an Orientation Unit, which aims to prepare students for the course they are about to follow. There is a quiz that tests their aptitude for language learning in an amusing but scientifically-

based way, and two tests that are designed to diagnose their linguistic strengths and weaknesses.

Generally speaking, the other units in *Headway Advanced* have nine sections, though not always in the same order. These are
  – a discussion point to launch the theme of the unit
  – one or more reading texts
  – two vocabulary exercises
  – a listening text
  – a speaking/discussion/roleplay activity
  – a suggestion for extended writing
  – the Language study, where students are either given the rules of the target language or challenged to work them out for themselves, and where the target language is practised
  – a revision section, which is sometimes related to the other areas of input and sometimes not.

The Language study is cross-referenced to the Grammar section at the back of the book, where the target language is explained in more depth.

There is some pronunciation work in the units, but this is mainly dealt with in the Workbook. The writing input (for example, linking devices, cause and result, formal and informal style) is in the Workbook also. The Language study section is cued after the reading and listening texts. This is to ensure a balance in the timetable of accuracy and fluency based activities.

Accuracy versus fluency

There has been much debate in recent years about the amount of attention that should be paid to the language in parts as opposed to the language as a whole. The premise of the debate is that the isolation of a component part (for example, the Future Continuous, giving opinions, or rules of sentence stress) and its controlled practice does not lead to mastery of the item when put back with the whole. Research has suggested that students perhaps learn the forms of a language best when their attention is on the meaning.

This debate is probably impossible to resolve, because we can never know the ideal ratio for all levels and all students. Students learn in different ways, and the constraints on low-level teaching mean that extensive fluency work is out of the question. No doubt both accuracy and fluency based activities have a place in the timetable at all levels. In theory, the more students are exposed to real language and are asked to do real things with the language they possess, the more their confidence should grow. For this reason, in *Headway Intermediate* there is more fluency work than accuracy work. After the intermediate level, however, the problem can be seen in different ways. It could be argued that at the upper-intermediate level, less time should be devoted to accuracy work and more to fluency work, thus exposing students to ever more 'real' language. Somehow or other, they acquire more language and become more accurate, so that at an advanced level, little or no accuracy work is necessary at all.

Alternatively, it could be argued that after the intermediate level, the amount of accuracy work should increase. If students have a certain grasp of basic grammar and vocabulary, and the confidence to use it, then now is the time to work on many of the other areas of the language where mistakes are made but which do not impede communication. In *Headway Upper-Intermediate*, there is more accuracy than fluency work, and this trend is continued in *Headway Advanced*. Students at this level do not want to be fluent and inaccurate. They want their performance to be as near as possible to that of a native speaker. For this reason, there is a lot of work on revising and extending the students' grasp of grammar and building their vocabulary in both the Student's Book and the Workbook.

Accuracy work

Grammatical syllabus

The grammatical areas dealt with consist of items that will be revision, such as narrative tenses, relative clauses and modal verbs of obligation, and items that students might not have consciously considered before, such as ellipsis (leaving words out), the future in the past, nouns in groups, the subjunctive, and ways of adding emphasis. Students at this level should be able to cope with quite complex areas such as the difference between **will**, **must** and **should** to express possibility about the present, and tense usage to express fact versus non-fact. It is certainly the time to examine many smaller areas of the language that are not particularly high frequency, and which before this level are perhaps not worth pointing out to students. Examples of these are **as** versus **like**, reflexive pronouns, adjective order, adverbs with two forms (**most**; **mostly**,) and nouns with a special meaning in the plural (**minute**; **minutes**).

There is an overview of the tense system at the beginning of the book. By the end of Unit 5, students have worked on past tenses, future forms, the passive voice and the perfect aspect.

Vocabulary syllabus

Vocabulary work is given a prominent place in *Headway Advanced*. There are at least two vocabulary exercises per unit in the Student's Book, and crossword puzzles and further input in the Workbook. There is a three-pronged approach to vocabulary development:

1 Encouraging effective vocabulary learning habits. As there is so much vocabulary in a language, and students' needs and interests vary, it is important that the students themselves assume a certain responsibility for their vocabulary acquisition. They should be very strongly encouraged to keep vocabulary records, and to review these records regularly. In the Orientation Unit, there is work on the organization of a dictionary entry and the information that can be gleaned from it, and dictionary work is encouraged throughout the course.

2 Introducing students to the systems of vocabulary. This is important because it shows that the words of a language are not isolated and unrelated, but can be part of a pattern, which, if perceived, can act as a 'peg' for learning.
Examples of these systems are synonyms and their associations, homophones, heterophones (words with the same spelling but different pronunciation and meaning, such as 'contract and con'tract), euphemisms, homonyms, slang, and multi-word nouns. Synonyms are given particular attention, as English is very rich in them. This is one of the reasons why English has the largest vocabulary of any language.

3 Introducing students to new words. This is, of course, important, but it is by no means as generative as the above two.

It is perhaps worth mentioning that the above strategies are all conscious means of acquiring vocabulary, but one of the most 'painless' ways of learning new words is by reading as much as possible.

The Workbook

The Workbook consists almost entirely of accuracy-based exercises, and is for classroom use as well as homework. The target structures of the Student's Book are further practised, and are sometimes expanded. For example, in Unit 2, there are exercises on narrative tenses, followed by an explanation of **would** versus **used to** to express past habit, and an exercise to practise it. In Unit 9, there is an exercise which aims to highlight students' awareness of the fundamental difference between defining and non-defining relative clauses, which you might want to use as an introduction to the area. So it is worth looking at the exercises in the Workbook before beginning a unit in the Student's Book, to see what material you might want to incorporate into your timetable.

In addition to the practice of the target structures of the Student's Book, there are a number of other threads in the Workbook. These are:

- at least one pronunciation exercise per unit
- a writing input (which could be used in class), and/or a suggestion for extended writing for each unit

- an exercise on multi-word verbs in the first and in every even-numbered unit. This is not just vocabulary input but aims to build students' understanding of how they operate and how to use them. In Unit 2, the four types of multi-word verb are presented, and there is an explanation of how a dictionary entry tells you which type a verb is; in Unit 4, the exercise shows how the literal and non-literal uses of a multi-word verb can be related.
- an exercise on idioms in every odd-numbered unit. In some cases, the aim is to give the origin of the idiom.
- an exercise on preposition collocations in every odd-numbered unit. The correct use of prepositions can cause students many problems.
- an extra reading in every even-numbered unit, with gaps, to be used as a comprehension and vocabulary exercise.
- a crossword puzzle in every third unit, to check vocabulary learning.
- three appendixes at the back of the Workbook, on multi-word verbs, dependent prepositions and linking words.

Note that there is no Orientation unit in the Workbook. The Workbook starts at Unit 1.

Fluency work

We have tried to select topics and material that will interest a thoughtful adult of any background. We have included several extracts from English literature, as in our experience students derive immense pleasure from this. The majority of the listening texts consist of interviews with well-known personalities or experts in their own fields, so there should be an inherent interest-value in what they are saying. We hope the material will be thought-provoking and sometimes controversial. Don't forget the many sources of supplementary ideas and material. Students should be strongly encouraged to do as much reading as possible, as it is potentially the cheapest and one of the most enjoyable ways of learning a language. You could either all buy the same book to read at home and discuss in class, or start a class library.

It can be very interesting to ask students to read aloud in class. At lower levels, this can be rather unproductive if a student's pronunciation is so bad that nobody can understand, but this shouldn't be such a problem with an advanced class. Some of the reading texts in *Headway Advanced* lend themselves to this, and this is indicated in the notes on the units.

It can be very useful to invite guest speakers into your class, to talk about almost anything! There is an element of live content in what a speaker has to say, and it takes the focus off the language and onto the content. Similarly, you could record programmes from the television and radio if you have the equipment. Finally, talks are a good way of providing extended listening practice for students, as well as provoking discussion. Students can take it in turns to talk for three or four minutes either on a topic of their choice (a book or film they've enjoyed, a place they have visited, a period in history that interests them, etc.) or a prescribed topic. Again, this gives the element of real content to a classroom lesson, which can otherwise sometimes be artificial and uninspiring.

We hope you enjoy using Headway Advanced!

ORIENTATION

What makes a good language learner?

OVERVIEW OF THE UNIT

- As you begin *Headway Advanced*, you are probably beginning a new course, possibly with a new group of students. In which case, your main aim will be *introductions*, and discussing together the aims and priorities of the course to come.

- The aim of the Orientation Unit is also introduction, although it is quite suitable for a continuing class. It is intended to take approximately four hours of classroom time, although this could be reduced or extended to suit your timetable. The quiz encourages students to examine their own strategies for language learning, and although the tone is light-hearted, the content is serious. In the ensuing discussion, students should be able to swap ideas with their colleagues.

- The aim of the Vocabulary work and the Language study is partly diagnostic and partly to *get down to work* as soon as possible. Students need to be aware of the range of information a dictionary can provide, and an ability to recognize the phonemic script is extremely useful. You need to know your students' linguistic strengths and weaknesses, as do they, in order to work on them.

NOTES ON THE UNIT

- Before beginning the unit, make sure students are familiar with the organization of the book. Each unit (except the Orientation Unit) is usually divided into the following sections.
  - Discussion
  - Reading
  - Vocabulary 1
  - Vocabulary 2
  - Listening
  - Speaking/Discussion/Roleplay
  - Writing
  - Language study
  - Revision

Point out the Grammar Section and the Tapescript Section at the back of the Student's Book, and perhaps ask them how these could be used for study outside class. Familiarity with the organization should enable students to perceive the aims of each activity, and allow them to revise from material already covered.

● Quiz   (SB 6)

- Introduction: tell your students that this is a quiz to find out their aptitude for language learning.

- Do the quiz all together, taking it in turns to read the questions out loud. Then students choose their answers.

- Try to keep up a momentum. Monitor students carefully to see when they are ready to move on. Some questions are very quick to answer, and some need to be timed (questions 12 and 13).

- Go through the answers all together with students adding up their scores as they go along. The answers are printed on page 7 of the student's book.

- Students read the appropriate interpretation.

● Discussion   (SB 7)

- Students answer questions 1 – 3 of the discussion in small groups.
  If the discussion is going on well in groups, you could ask them to answer questions 4 – 6 as well.
  Alternatively, get the feedback to the first three questions, then discuss the final three all together.

Sample answers
(Obviously there are no set answers for question 1.)
2 The quiz in fact highlights many of the characteristics

that theorists tell us the good learner possesses. He/she is:

- *confident in his/her ability to learn*
- *self-reliant*
- *motivated and enthusiastic*
- *aware of why he/she wants to learn*
- *unafraid of making mistakes, and unafraid of what he/she doesn't know*
- *a good risk-taker*
- *a good guesser*
- *probably positive in his/her attitude to English language and culture*
- *a good pattern perceiver*
- *prepared to look for opportunities to come into contact with the language*
- *willing to assume a certain responsibility for learning.*

3 *Gesture (shrugging shoulders); exclamations/noises (Uh! to express surprise; Phew! to express relief); deaf and dumb sign language; morse code; sign languages conducted by flags or mirrors reflecting the sun.*

4 *A difficult question, and you might need to explain it further. When learning a foreign language, you are to a certain extent leaving behind the security of your own language and you become a 'child' again, starting 'from scratch'. The risk-taker doesn't mind trying to get a message across, even though he/she knows that mistakes will be made, and isn't put off by not understanding everything that he/she reads or listens to.*

5 *It has been suggested that women might be better language learners than men because they are more interested in people and go out to them more readily. They are less afraid of making mistakes which might make them feel a little foolish. Men are more aware of their status in a group, would rather hold back and say nothing, and certainly do not want to appear foolish. These are somewhat extreme viewpoints, but are nevertheless interesting!*

6 *The obvious conclusion is that the extrovert who is prepared to go out to people and find opportunities to interact will learn more quickly. This requires confidence and sociability. Researchers are hesitant to commit themselves, however, because personality is difficult to identify and measure. People are confident in some things and not others, for example.*

● Vocabulary (SB 8)

- Introduction: this is to check that students know how a dictionary entry is organized and check they can recognize the phonemic symbols.

It might seem rather late in a student's language learning career to work on the organization of a dictionary entry and the phonetic symbols. However, students may have been using a dictionary for years

and only extracting a limited amount of the information that a dictionary provides. They may not have realized that different type-faces are used for definitions, examples, idioms (and compounds); that information about a word comes in a certain order; that many symbols are used to cross-refer and explain. All this information would probably have overwhelmed them earlier in their learning, but at the advanced level they should be ready to absorb all the information a dictionary provides.

You can expect some students to be very familiar with the phonetic symbols, and others to have no experience of them whatsoever. This all depends on their previous learning. Reassure those who know nothing about them that they only need to be able to recognize the symbols, not produce them, and that by and large the symbols are very logical and simple.

1 The organization of a dictionary entry (SB 8)

- Students do exercise 1 in pairs, then check the answers all together.

2 Pronunciation (SB 9)

- Ask students to take it in turns to read aloud the example words for the vowels, diphthongs and consonants on the chart of phonetic symbols. Then ask others to say just the sound in isolation. Students can find this quite difficult.

1 Students work in pairs to do question 1, practising the words and sounds.

2 Students work in pairs to do question 2, identifying the vowel sounds.

Answers

bread 3,	steak 13,	suit 9,	fear 18,
wear 19,	hut 10,	wood 8,	bath 5,
rose 14,	noise 17,	round 16,	chip 2,
cheap 1,	ham 4,	more 7,	wise 15,
bird 11,	fox 6		

Practice (SB 9)

- Ask a student to read out loud the introduction. You could ask your class how they say **buzz** and **snore** in their language. Many of the words in this exercise are examples of onomatopoeia, but not all of them. **To slouch**, for example, does not involve any noise, but it sounds lazy and heavy! (Onomatapoeia is further dealt with in Unit 8.)

1 Students work in three groups to decide the spelling of the words. Each group should work on one column only. The feedback could be conducted as a class activity, or with a representative from each group.

Answers

thump	*mumble*	*giggle*
munch	*scratch*	*smooth*
sniff	*scrape*	*squeeze*
squeamish	*miaou/miaow*	*slouch*
slimy	*howl*	*sluggish*
grumble	*gargle*	*wobble*

Check the concept of the words by asking questions such as:

Why do you thump someone?
What sort of food do you munch? (apples)
Think of two reasons why people sniff. (got a cold; crying)
What are you squeamish about?
Are fish slimy?
What do people grumble about? (weather; paying tax)
Can you hear someone who mumbles?
What animals scratch?
What vegetables do you have to scrape? (carrots; potatoes)

Students find the words **scratch** and **scrape** hard to differentiate. You scratch yourself on a rose bush – the mark is long and thin. If you fall over while you are running, you might scrape your knees – the marks are over a surface. Ask students what the difference is between scraping your car and scratching your car.

Which animals howl?
Why do people gargle? What with? (antiseptic; mouthwash)
Who often giggle? (schoolgirls)
What's a baby's skin like? What about a man's unshaven face?
What can you squeeze? (someone's hand; a lemon) Why?
Ask a student to slouch in his/her chair, and ask How do you feel? (tired; bored)
What colour is a slug? How do slugs move?
Why do people feel sluggish in the morning?
What food that children like wobbles? (jelly)
Why might your legs wobble? (afraid, ill, exhausted, shocked)

– Don't let the question of what the words sound like go on too long. Just three or four examples should be enough.

Answers

None of the words sound particularly pleasant, but many of them sound unpleasant (slimy, grumble, sluggish)! Thump sounds short-lasting; howl sounds long-lasting. Miaou and giggle sound high-pitched; thump and grumble sound low-pitched.

2 Students work in pairs to fill the gaps or answer the questions.

Answers

a. *thumping*
b. *sniffing*
c. *scrape*
d. *slimy*
e. *scratch*
f. *squeamish*
g. *smooth*

– Students work in pairs to prepare further sentences then test their colleagues.

LANGUAGE STUDY   (SB 10)

Either or both of the exercises in the Language study could be set as homework to be checked in class. However, we suggest that Exercise 1 is done in class as students benefit from peer co-operation in deciding the correct tense or verb form, and much valuable discussion ensues on the grammatical areas tested.

---

1 Tenses and verb forms   (SB 10)

– Students work in groups of two or three to decide the correct tense or verb form.

Answers

a. *I haven't seen you . . . What have you been doing . . . I last saw you*
b. *I'm looking forward . . . spring arriving . . . Winter seems to have been . . . I can't stand getting up . . . some flowers should be coming*
c. *I arrived . . . Someone had forgotten to turn off . . . water had poured/had been pouring out . . . Before phoning . . . I checked to see . . . I didn't want there to be*
d. *I wish you had told me . . . you didn't like fruit cake . . . I would have made . . . What am I going to do*
e. *in case it rains . . . forecast said it would/was going to get . . . I'd wrap up well*
f. *I might have liked it . . . teachers had been kind . . . my children are old enough to go . . . they are going to/are going to go to/they will go to (The first one is best.)*
g. *I haven't been . . . Since we moved . . . we have been busy decorating . . . I wanted . . . I've lost*
h. *The Azra Trading Company was taken over . . . Azra has lost . . . he hoped that Azra would soon be*
i. *I intended to finish writing . . . I didn't have*
j. *I was going out/was going to go out . . . I have just heard . . . the production has been cancelled . . . I suppose I'll just stay*

2 Correcting mistakes   (SB 10-11)

– The mistakes in this exercise are of a general nature. Students find some of them easy to correct, but some are quite subtle and will need careful explanation. In the answers below, there are some notes to help you. We suggest students do this exercise for homework, then check their answers together in small groups before you check their answers as a class. Students will inevitably ask many questions, wanting to know if their answers are possible and what the difference is between x and y.

Answers

Dear Anna
Thank you for your letter, which came yesterday. (**That** is not possible. **which came yesterday** is a non-defining relative clause, so **which** is used and there must be a comma. **which came yesterday** is extra, incidental information. Serge is not saying 'Thank you for the letter that came yesterday as opposed to the one that came three days ago'.)

I do like to hear/hearing from you. (**Do** adds emphasis. When the verb **like** expresses a general preference, it can be followed by either the infinitive or the -ing form.) *The news of your interview is very interesting. You didn't say if you got the job.* (**Work** is general, and is usually uncountable.) *I hope so. I was sorry to hear that you had/have been burgled again. How many times has this happened to you? Five hundred pounds is a lot of money.* (**Five hundred pounds** is seen as a unit, not as five hundred separate pound coins, so is followed by a singular verb.) *Do the police know who did it?* (**who** is the subject of the indirect question.) *You wanted me to tell you about what I am doing in Edinburgh, and what my life is like here.* (**How is it?** is not possible when it means – 'Describe it to me generally'.) *Well, I'm enjoying it very much.* (**Enjoy** is a transitive verb, and needs an object.) *The course is good, but harder than I thought. At first, I didn't have any friends* (**At first** means **in the beginning; first** begins a list. The Past Simple negative of **have** as a full verb is **didn't have; hadn't** is mainly used as an auxiliary verb only.) *but I soon got to know the people who are in the same department as me. At the moment,* (**Actually** means in fact.) *I'm spending the whole time/all my time trying to buy the books I need/that I need* (**the books I need** is best. **I need** defines which books.) *to read for my course, but it is difficult to find them.* (**Although** suggests a direct contrast of ideas. Here, **but** introduces a small problem.) *I'm sure I'll find them soon. When I've bought them, I'll be very busy!* (The Present Perfect is needed with **buy**, to show that the action of buying is completed before the next action begins.) *I'll finish now/I must finish now. A friend of mine has to write a letter in French, and I said I would help him. Write to me* (In British English, **write** needs

the preposition **to**; in American English it is possible to say **Write me**.) *or phone me soon.* (There is no preposition.) *If you come to Scotland, you must visit me,* (**Must** here expresses a strong recommendation, not an obligation.) *but remember to bring some warm clothes! It's such cold weather/it's so cold here!*

Best wishes,
Serge

UNIT 1

The best days of your life?

OVERVIEW OF THE UNIT

- The topic of education, its aims and systems, runs through this unit, with readings from Winston Churchill and A. S. Neill, and a jigsaw listening on independent schools in Britain. Education is a subject that affects us all, and one which students generally find interesting. Students are asked to comment on their own previous learning, and to discuss what the priorities of the ideal school should be.

- In the vocabulary work, there is the first of many exercises in the book on synonyms in English. It has often been said that English has the largest vocabulary of any language because it admits and allows so many near synonyms, and an ability to recognize and produce these will greatly enrich a student's performance. It has also been said that there are no true synonyms, as shades of meaning, differences of use or collocation mean that no two words completely overlap.

NOTES ON THE LANGUAGE INPUT

Noun phrases

Four ways of adding information to a noun are highlighted.

- plural expressions before a noun
  a five-hour journey
- compound nouns
  house plants
- prepositional phrases
  a man with a parrot on his shoulder
- participle clauses
  a house overlooking the Thames

Avoiding repetition

Two aspects of avoiding repetition are dealt with. When an auxiliary verb is used on its own (without a main

verb) because the main verb has been used before, it is an example of ellipsis.

She said she'd come, but she hasn't.

If there is no auxiliary verb, **do/does/did** is used, and this is an example of substitution. Students are familiar with substitution in structures such as short answers, tag questions, and structures with **so** and **neither**.
She went to university, and I did, too.
'You don't like me, do you?' 'Yes, I do.'
'John plays golf.' 'So does my sister.'
'I don't smoke.' 'Neither do I.'

NOTES ON THE UNIT

● Discussion (SB 13)

- Introduction: Ask students what they think the title of the unit means. School days are sometimes referred to as the best days of your life. Ask questions such as:
  Why might school days be referred to as the best days of your life?
  Do you agree?
  Were they for you?
  Did you enjoy your school days?
  What sort of school did you go to?

- Students read the chart showing the organization of state education in England, then work in pairs or small groups to prepare questions to ask you. Make sure their questions are well-formed. Obviously, you cannot be expected to know everything about state education in Britain, so don't worry if there are questions you don't know the answer to, but here are some notes to help you.

The responsibility for education is distributed between central government, local education authorities (LEAs) and the governing bodies of the schools.

5

Nursery education is voluntary. Some LEAs provide nursery education, or have reception classes in primary schools which last from 9 a.m. to 3 p.m. There are some private sector nursery schools, which parents pay for.

Secondary education

About 5% of pupils go to independent (private) schools. Of the remainder, the vast majority (90%) attend comprehensive schools. These began in the 1950s, and admit children without reference to ability or aptitude. The children represent a total social cross-section, and all the subjects are available. In a very few areas, children are selected according to levels of academic attainment, and depending on their results in an exam (the 11+), go either to a grammar school, which runs academic courses for selected pupils aged 11-18, or to a secondary modern, which offers a more general education for pupils up to 16, although they can stay on if they wish.

Exams

The exams that pupils take used to be as follows: GCE (General Certificate of Education) O Level (Ordinary), taken at 16 in a number of subjects (average six). CSE (Certificate of Secondary Education), also taken at 16, but easier than O Level. GCE A Level (Advanced), taken at 18 in fewer subjects, usually 1, 2, 3 or 4.

In 1988, O Levels and CSEs were phased out and replaced with GCSEs (General Certificate of Secondary Education), taken at 16. These are more practical, with less emphasis on retaining facts and more on the application of them. Assessment is continuous, with at least 20% of coursework counting towards the final grade. A Levels continue unchanged.

Curriculum

The curriculum is decided by the LEAs and the school governing body, although the government is moving towards national criteria for syllabuses. Schools must provide teaching in English, mathematics, science, religious education, physical education, humanities, some practical and some aesthetic activity. Most pupils learn a foreign language.

After 16

About 50% of children continue their education after 16, some in schools, others in colleges of further education and technical colleges. For entrance to a university, pupils need at least two A levels, but usually universities ask for three. About 5% of children go to university. Courses usually last for three years, at the end of which students are awarded a degree (Bachelor of Arts, Bachelor of Science). Postgraduate degrees are MA (Master of Arts), MSc (Master of Science) and PhD (Doctor of Philosophy).

Polytechnics offer academic subjects and training for particular jobs, which result in either a degree, a certificate or a diploma. They have close links with commerce and industry. Students receive grants for higher education from the LEAs, which are not repaid. The size of the grant depends on the student's or the parents' means. Student loans may be introduced shortly and may eventually replace grants.

– Discuss the remaining questions as a class.

● Reading (SB 14)

– Introduction: tell students that they will read an extract from Winston Churchill's autobiography, and ask them what they know about him.

Winston Churchill started his career as a soldier, fighting in India and Egypt. Politically he started as a Liberal. He held many government posts and finally became Prime Minister of a coalition government in 1940. During World War II, his remarkable ability as an orator and qualities as leader made him a symbol of British resistance to tyranny. He was largely responsible for Britain's alliance with the Soviet Union and the USA in 1941, but came to view Soviet communism as a future threat, speaking later of an 'iron curtain' drawn across Europe. His government was defeated in 1945, but he returned as Conservative Prime Minister from 1951–55.

– Students discuss their first school in pairs or small groups, then read the text.

Notes on the text
line 5   **the very last thing in schools** We would nowadays say **the very latest thing**
line 6   **swimming pond** nowadays we say **pool**
line 9   **mortar-board** stiff, black cap with a flat, square top and a tassle hanging from it
line 10   **hamper** a large basket containing food
line 27   **three half-crowns** Before decimalization in Britain in 1971, there used to be 240 pennies to the pound, or eight half-crowns. A halfcrown was 30 old pennies, ($12\frac{1}{2}$ present-day pennies).

Comprehension check (SB 15)

– Students work in pairs or small groups to answer the Comprehension check questions.

Answers

1 *The school was seemingly most attractive, offering everything one could want, but he felt extremely miserable.*
2 *Spilling his cup and making a bad start; being left alone with strangers; the building was formidable; having lessons all day*

3 *He gave them to the Headmaster, who said that there would be a shop at the school.*

4 *Because the Form Master didn't explain what Latin was, what a declension was or what the Latin words meant – he just told Churchill to learn it. He probably knew that Latin was a classical language, but not that it had nouns and declensions.*

5 *Because he thought Churchill was being impertinent, and not just genuinely curious to learn.*

6 *miserable; fierce; formidable; bleak; gloomy; aching heart; rigmarole; sorrows*

– Ask two students to act out the dialogue between the Form Master and Churchill, beginning at line 61. Appoint another student as the narrator.

– Repeat this activity with students working in groups of three. Monitor pronunciation, especially intonation, carefully.

What do you think? (SB 15)

– Answer the 'What do you think?' questions as a class.

▶ **Language focus** (SB 20 TB 10)

● Vocabulary 1 (SB 16)

– Students are introduced to an important feature of English vocabulary, which is the fact that it has many synonyms.

– Introduction: Ask students to guess how many words there are in the English language.

> There are about 60,000 words in common use. The *Oxford Advanced Learner's Dictionary* boasts 57,100 words and phrases as headwords. In addition most areas of life have their own specialized vocabulary. The *Oxford English Dictionary* has 290,000 headwords. This includes alternative spellings but does not include all of the thousands of derivatives. An informed guess puts the number of lexical items in the English language at 500-600,000. You could explain that one reason why there are so many synonyms in English is that English has borrowed from its various invaders, Anglo-Saxon (Germanic) and French.

– You might choose to do exercise 1 and 2 in separate sessions, otherwise students might be overwhelmed by too many words.

1 Synonyms in context (SB 16)

– Students read the introduction to exercise 1 then work in pairs to answer the questions. Lexicons would be very useful for this exercise.

Answers

a. *talented, accomplished, gifted*
b. *convincing*
c. *correspondence*
d. *disability, handicap*
e. *curb, check, manage, cut down, reduce, limit*
f. *deceive, mislead*
g. *breakthroughs, advances, improvements*
h. *direction, leadership*
i. *strategies, moves*
j. *thorough (detailed cannot be used for a medical examination)*

Synonyms and their associations (SB 16)

– Students work in pairs to find synonyms and write sentences to explore their associations. Rather than asking *all* students to look up *all* the words, you could allocate two words to five groups, for example, who then explore their words and give feedback to the rest of the class.

Answers

a. *ally, in war; partner, in business or sport; colleague, at work; comrade, in socialism; companion, on a journey; mate, pal, chum, buddy are informal.*
b. *speak; utter a sound, an unkind word; preach a sermon; chat; gossip; debate a problem; make a speech*
c. *glance at the newspaper headlines; peep through a keyhole; peer through the darkness; scan the horizon; survey the scene; gaze into space, into someone's eyes; stare at someone on the bus; glare in anger*
d. *nervous before an exam; apprehensive about what might happen; anxious about someone's well-being; scared of spiders*
e. *adore one's mother; worship God; revere someone's memory; idolize a pop star*
f. *loathe the sight of something; dislike food; detest someone; can't bear/stand something/someone; abhor*
g. *fracture a bone; shatter a glass; smash a window; wreck a car; demolish a building; crack a cup; ruin*
h. *repair a bike; patch trousers; restore a painting; fix a leaking tap; darn a sock*
i. *appealing idea; tempting offer; seductive eyes; charming person; delightful children; pretty girl; handsome man*
j. *insane, lunatic, crazy person or idea; nuts, crackers, out of one's mind*

● Listening (SB 16)

T.1a/b **Pre-listening task** (SB 16)

– Do question 1 of the pre-listening task as a class, and question 2 with students working in pairs. Check that the questions are well-formed.

Jigsaw listening (SB 17)

– Students divide into two groups to listen to the different texts and answer the questions. They might want to listen twice.

> This activity ideally uses two cassette recorders and two cassettes. If only one is available either assign other work to one group while the other group listens or consider letting one group read the script rather than listen.

– Students pair up with someone from the other group and compare answers. As with all jigsaw activities, the students have very different information, so there is a lot to explain, listen to and ask about.

Answers

1 *Dr Beer explains that the name started because before state education was available to all, public schools were indeed open to the public. They prefer the word independent nowadays because they are independent of government control. Patricia Wilby says that they prefer the name independent because it suggests initiative and enterprise instead of snobbery and prejudice.*

2 *Dr Beer says uniforms and manners have not changed, but the curriculum has changed a lot. Science is taught, as well as craft design technology, Russian, and computer sciences. According to Patricia Wilby, what is remarkable is not so much what has changed but the fact that the changes happened so recently, for example, changes in the curriculum, abolishing fagging (a system where a younger boy does jobs for an older boy) only in 1980, and admitting pupils from a cross-section of society. She says that some things have not changed, for example, the fact that the majority of top jobs are filled by people who went to public school.*

3 *Dr Beer says the curriculum has changed fundamentally. Although the classics are still taught, the subjects are modern and relevant. Patricia Wilby also says that the curriculum has changed a lot, and that engineering is the largest destination for public-school leavers. Science and computer studies are important. Independent schools have tried to bury the image of being obsessed with the classics and sporting achievement.*

4 *Patricia Wilby stresses that academic success is vital. Dr Beer says they try to educate the whole man, and this means activities other than academic ones.*

5 *Dr Beer says boys are not beaten any more, but anti-social behaviour is punished by having to perform a social duty. Patricia Wilby says that at Oundle, another public school, boys have not been beaten for many years.*

6 *Dr Beer says that his school is like a village, but it sounds like a self-contained village with little contact with the people outside in the rest of the town of Harrow, although some boys were punished by having to pick up litter in the public streets of Harrow. Patricia Wilby says that what makes the British system unique is the extent to which it is set apart from the rest of the nation. This is because by comparison, the private sector in Britain is small.*

What do you think? (SB 17)

– Answer the 'What do you think?' questions as a class.

● Reading (SB 18)

– Introduction: Ask students what they understand by 'alternative' schools, and if they know of any.

– Look at the picture of A. S. Neill and his students, and discuss how you think life is different at Summerhill. Students read the first part of the text.

– Ask students for their reactions to the first part of the text. A. S. Neill's ideas are quite remarkable, so students should have something to say. Ask if they would have liked such a school, and to what extent they feel Summerhill prepares pupils for the real world.

Questions for prediction (SB 18)

– Students discuss the questions for prediction. There are, of course, no set answers for these. They serve to check students' understanding of the kind of school Summerhill is, and to motivate them to read the next part of the text.

Questions for discussion (SB 19)

– Do the questions for discussion as a class. A lively discussion should ensue, as A. S. Neill makes comments not just about education but about society and the quality of life.

▶ **Language focus** (SB 21 TB 10)

● Writing (SB 19)

– Students write about one of the subjects for homework.

● Discussion (SB 19)

Groupwork (SB 19)

– Students work in groups of four to complete column A. They usually end up agreeing with each other within their group, but this is not necessary for the activity.

– Monitor the groups carefully to see when they have finished.

Work alone (SB 19)

Ask them to work alone to complete column B.

Pairwork (SB 19)

– Students work in pairs to complete column C.

– Compare your conclusions as a class. When there are differences of opinion, ask for justifications.

● Vocabulary 2 (SB 20)

– English spelling is, of course, notoriously irregular, which explains why the same vowel sound can be spelt in several different ways, and why there are so many homophones in English.

1 Spelling and pronunciation (SB 20)

– Students work in pairs to put the twenty-five words into the correct column.

> For those students who are unfamiliar with the phonetic symbols you could put a word with that vowel sound on the board.
> /eɪ/ lay /e/ bed
> /ɔː/ for /aɪ/ mine
> /ɜː/ word /iː/ seem
> /uː/ mood

– Students will naturally not all finish Exercise 1 at the same time so those that finish first can be asked to do Exercise 2 Homophones.

– When everyone has finished Exercise 1, ask one student to read out his/her columns to check that everyone agrees.

> Words that often cause trouble are **sword**, **fur**, **bury** and **suite**, and the /s/ or /z/ at the end of **praise** /z/, **raise** /z/, **course** /s/, **pause** /z/, **sauce** /s/, **bruise** /z/, **crews** /z/ and **seize** /z/, so correct any mistakes vigilantly.

Answers

/eɪ/	/ɔː/
weight	*course*
praise	*pause*
paste	*caught*
waste	*sauce*
rain	*sword*
raise	*floor*
	hall

/ɜː/	/uː/
fur	*bruise*
heard	*crews*
/e/	/aɪ/
bury	*isle*
bread	*sight*

/iː/
seize
peal
key
suite

2 Homophones (SB 20)

– Students work in groups to think of the homophones. This can be quite difficult. Even though they often know the other word, they don't associate the two pronunciations, so if they get stuck, tell them to move on.

Answers

weight	*wait*	*course*	*coarse*
praise	*prays*	*pause*	*paws*
paste	*paced*	*caught*	*court*
waste	*waist*	*sauce*	*source*
rain	*reign*	*sword*	*sawed*
raise	*rays*	*floor*	*flaw*
		hall	*haul*

fur	*fir*	*bruise*	*brews*
heard	*herd*	*crews*	*cruise*

bury	*berry*	*isle*	*aisle, I'll*
bread	*bred*	*sight*	*site*

seize	*sees, seas*
peal	*peel*
key	*quay*
suite	*sweet*

– Test the above words by asking questions:

What's the verb from weight?
What's the noun from pray?
Tell me some kinds of paste. (toothpaste, tomato paste)
How long has Queen Elizabeth II reigned?
What rays do you know? (the sun, X-rays)
What is the opposite of coarse material? What is a coarse joke?
If a vase has a flaw in it, what's the matter?
What nouns go with haul? (a haul of fish, drugs, stolen goods)
What berries do you know? (strawberry, blackberry, raspberry, blueberry)
What's the infinitive of bred? (breed)
Where's the aisle in a church? (the gap between rows of seats)

If you take someone down the aisle, what do you do?
(marry them)
What needs to be peeled before you can eat it?
(orange, potato)

3 Rhymes   (SB 20)

You will probably want to do this third exercise in a separate session from the first two. Do it the next day, or a few days later, to act as revision.

Sample answers

weight – late, hate, eight
course – horse, force
praise – weighs, phase, haze
waste – chaste, laced
rain – wane, mane, brain
raise – see praise
pause – laws, chores, bores, roars
caught – fought, sought, fort, nought
sauce – see course
sword – bored, gnawed, lord
floor – more, gore, law, lore
haul – ball, drawl
fur – whirr, sir.
heard – word, bird
bruise – lose, choose
crews – see bruise
bury – very, merry
bread – head, said, wed
isle – file, while, trial
sight – might, light, height
seize – keys, peas, breeze
key – free, me
suite – beat, meat, feet

LANGUAGE STUDY   (SB 20)

1 Noun phrases   (SB 20)

– Students find examples of compound nouns, prepositional phrases and participle clauses in 'Winston Churchill's Prep School' SB 14.

Answers
Compound nouns

swimming pond
football and cricket grounds
school treats
November afternoon
steam engine
Form Room

Prepositional phrases

boys in a class
M.A.s in gowns and mortar-boards

fear of spilling
idea of being left
collection of soldiers
sound of my mother's departing wheels

Participle clauses

everything provided by the authorities
apartments reserved for the instruction and accommodation of the pupils
book filled with words

– Students could read the Grammar section for homework, or in class, as it is quite short.

▶ **Grammar reference:**   (SB 134)

– Students do the Practice exercise in pairs.

Practice   (SB 21)

– Students do the exercise in pairs.

Answers

a. *He bought an eighty-thousand-pound farmhouse with three acres of land.*
b. *A twelve-year-old girl wearing a clown's outfit came into the room.*
c. *I need some six-inch steel nails.*
d. *Concorde is the fastest passenger plane in the world.*
e. *Have you seen those Swiss army knives with gadgets for everything?*
f. *She is a much-respected economics lecturer at Bristol University.*
g. *She has just started a fifteen-thousand-pound job with/for a New York firm of accountants.*
h. *He bought a three-hundred-year-old picture of two men working in a field.*
i. *We had a splendid four-course meal with two bottles of wine for less than fifteen pounds.*
j. *It was a long, twelve-hour flight with stop-overs in Delhi and Moscow.*
k. *The forty-car pile-up on the M1, caused by yesterday's freak weather conditions, has finally been cleared by police.*
l. *Pan Am Airways passengers flying to New York can expect three-hour delays.*

2 Avoiding repetition   (SB 21)

– Read the explanation on avoiding repetition as a class.

Practice   (SB 21)

– Students do this exercise in pairs.

Answers

a. *I couldn't*
b. *I am*
c. *I have/did*

10

d. *I will*
e. *we hadn't*
f. *I haven't I will*
g. *it does*
h. *it was/were*
i. *she would have*
j. *I would*
k. *You should*
l. *he would*
m. *I hadn't*
n. *he wouldn't*
o. *We might*
p. *He would* (**would** here expresses characteristic, annoying behaviour.)

– There is a further exercise on noun phrases in the Workbook.

▶ **Grammar reference:** (SB 134)

REVISION (SB 22)

1 'A' or 'an'? (SB 22)

– Students work in pairs to work out the rule of pronunciation in the first exercise.

> Most words beginning with **u–** are pronounced /ʌ/, but some are pronounced /juː/, in which case they do not begin with a vowel sound, and **a** is used, not **an**. Similarly with **h** – in most cases the **h** is pronounced, but in some cases it is silent, so **an** is used.

– Students can check the rules in the Grammar Section.

Answers

a university	*an MP*
a used car	*a UFO*
an honest man	*an uncle*
a human being	*an unfair result*
an X-ray	*an urgent message*
an umpire	*a unilateral declaration*
a European	*a united country*
a useful tool	

▶ **Grammar reference:** (SB 134)

2 'The' – /ðə/ or /ðɪ/? (SB 22)

Answers

Union Jack (1)
office (2)
air we breath (2)
heir to the throne (2)
USA (1)
universe (1)

Atlantic Ocean (2)
EEC (2)
UK (1)
MP for Leicester (2)
USSR (1)
English Channel (2)

university (1)
used car (1)
honest man (2)
human being (1)
X-ray (2)
umpire (2)
European (1)
useful tool (1)

MP (2)
UFO (1)
uncle (2)
unfair result (2)
urgent message (2)
unilateral declaration (1)
united country (1)

▶ **Grammar reference:** (SB 134)

EXTRA IDEAS

– For extra reading material, look in some autobiographies and biographies containing references to school-days. Roald Dahl's *Boy* is very good on the cruelties of public school life, and Laurie Lee's *Cider with Rosie* has some lovely passages about small country schools at the turn of the century.

– For extra listening material, record some of your English-speaking friends (on their own, or in a group) talking about the school they went to, or invite them into your class for half an hour. Students are often fascinated to hear about other people's schools, whether they liked it, how strict it was, the sort of tricks they got up to, etc. If you have a video, look out for documentaries on any aspect of education, or films which deal with schools or school-days.

– For extra speaking material, see if there are any topical issues to discuss. You could also have discussions or talks on the following subjects:

   – the case for private education
   – the case for state education
   – for and against physical punishment at school
   – boys benefit from mixed schools, but girls do better in single sex schools
   – the importance of sport
   – schools do not prepare us for life

UNIT 2

Literature

OVERVIEW OF THE UNIT

- There is a theme of literature running throughout the unit, with extracts from classical and popular fiction. This is partly to introduce students to a selection of English literature, but mainly to encourage them to read as much as possible. Reading is one of the easiest and most enjoyable ways of learning a language, so you should encourage it as much as possible. The importance of reading for pleasure is currently undergoing a reappraisal with some experts contending that it is a key factor in successfully mastering a language.

NOTES ON THE LANGUAGE INPUT

Narrative tenses

Students will be familiar with the Past Simple and Continuous and the Past Perfect Simple and Continuous, and this unit also introduces them to the future in the past. There is an examination of how these tenses are used to tell a story in chronological order, and how a writer uses them to 'look over his/her shoulder' and to preview events for dramatic effect.

Students may initially be surprised to learn that there are verb forms to express the future in the past, but a few examples and a little explanation should suffice. You could put the following sentences on the board and ask students to translate them, explaining how their language expresses this concept.

When Keith woke up on Thursday, he felt awful. He was seeing his bosses at 11.00, and he was sure they were going to sack him.

Was going to and the Past Continuous are the most common forms to express the future in the past in both the spoken and written language, but **would** is also used in a more literary context.

Harry ate lazily. Little did he know that this would be his last meal, and that by midnight he would be stone cold dead.

However, students will be familiar with a very similar use of **would**, and that is in indirect speech and thought.

He said he would come.
I thought she would win.

There is an exercise in the Workbook that explains and tests this area further.

Would used to express past habit is contrasted with **would** to express the future in the past.

NOTES ON THE UNIT

● **Discussion**   (SB 23)

'Characters from English literature'

- Look at the pictures of characters from English literature, and answer the questions as a class. Encourage those who know something about the authors or who have read the books to tell the others.

Here are some notes to help you:

Romeo and Juliet was Shakespeare's first romantic tragedy. It concerns the two chief families of Verona, the Montagues and the Capulets, who are bitter enemies. Romeo, the son of Lord Montague, falls in love with Juliet, Capulet's daughter. They marry in secret and commit suicide.

Gulliver's Travels was written by Jonathan Swift in 1726. It is a satire on contemporary politics and social mores. It is written in four parts, and in each part Gulliver visits a different land. In one (Lilliput), the people are all very small. In another (Brobdingnag) they are all very tall.

Sherlock Holmes was the creation of Arthur Conan Doyle, who wrote at the end of the last century and the beginning of this century. Holmes is a hawk-eyed amateur detective, whose brilliant solutions to a wide variety of crimes amaze everyone. He is aided and abetted by the stolid Dr Watson, with whom he shares rooms in Baker Street.

Alice in Wonderland was written by Lewis Carroll (1832-1898). He created the character of Alice to amuse a little girl called Alice Liddell. *Alice in Wonderland* recounts the adventures of a little girl in a make-believe world under the ground. Alice lands in this wonderland after she falls down a hole while following a rabbit. She meets many strange characters, including the Cheshire Cat, the Mad Hatter, the Queen of Hearts and the Mock Turtle. The book became so popular that the names of some of the characters are part of everyday speech, for example, *to grin like a Cheshire Cat*. There were further adventures for Alice in *Through the Looking-Glass*.

Oliver Twist was written by Charles Dickens, and was first published in 1837. Oliver Twist is the name given to a child of unknown parents born in a workhouse, and brought up in cruel conditions. He runs away to London and falls in with a band of thieves. He turns out to be the child of a wealthy family.

● Reading (SB 24)

- This examines the style, characters and content of different kinds of books.

Matching stories

- Students read the instructions. Make sure students know what they have to do, then ask them to work in pairs to match the beginnings and endings of the books. Encourage them to skim all the extracts quickly first.

   #### Answers
   1 and 4 are the autobiography.
   2 and 8 are the romance.
   5 and 3 are the fairy story.
   9 and 6 are the detective story.
   7 and 10 are the spy story.

- Ask students to read the extracts more carefully and discuss in pairs what helped them to match the extracts.

The autobiography is written in the first person, and is very factual, beginning as it does with time and place of birth. Although the ending could be fiction, it sounds like an old man or woman, nearing the end of his/her days, sitting nostalgically looking at the scenery.

The romance begins and ends with a man and a woman talking first about how much they don't love each other and finally about how much they do love each other. The style is very clichéd. The characters don't **speak**, they **snap** and **murmur**. The use of adjectives and adverbs is simplistic and hazily romantic – **tight lips; a long, sweet time; laughed softly; joined in gaily**. Comparing her spirit to the colour of her hair is strange, and the idea of his lips laying claim to her lips sounds like romantic colonialism.

Students have probably heard of the story of Cinderella. Children's stories often begin with **Once upon a time** and end with **And they all lived happily ever after**. They are filled with princes, princesses, kings and evil sisters.

The two extracts from the detective story both mention Mrs Ferrars. The books begins with a death and ends in a suicide. Poison is talked about, and students might know the detective Hercule Poirot from the many Agatha Christie films made.

Students will probably match the extracts from the spy story by a process of elimination rather than deduction. The style of the opening paragraph is clipped and considered. It talks about a recruit to a firm; a recruit suggests a military organization, while a firm is usually some kind of business enterprise.

The main clues are in the final extract, where Moscow is mentioned. It sounds as if the man is in Moscow, phoning his wife or girl-friend, and in a bad state. In fact he has defected.

Titles and authors (SB 25)

- Students match the titles and authors.

   #### Answers
   Autobiography – *My Autobiography*, by Charlie Chaplin
   Romance – *Marriage in Haste*, by Sue Peters
   Fairy story – *Cinderella*
   Detective story – *The Murder of Roger Ackroyd*, by Agatha Christie
   Spy story – *The Human Factor*, by Graham Greene

Kinds of books (SB 25)

- Students work in threes to talk about one kind of book. Try to get different groups working on different kinds, so that the range is covered. This should produce some quite light-hearted discussion, as students talk about typical ingredients and swap experiences of books they have read.

- The writing exercise is fun to do, but it takes longer than you might think for students to organize themselves and begin to write, so allow adequate time for this. You could give students a title from the following list to provide them with a definite starting point.

Detective stories
- Murder in the Vicarage
- Death comes at Midnight
- The Lady and the Tramp

Fairy story
- The Five Dwarfs
- The Princess and the Jester
- Jack and Jill in the Forest

Romance
- Love on the Ocean Wave
- Angels of Mercy
- Forbidden Love

Spy story
- The Mole
- The Berlin Gate
- The Day the President Defected

Science fiction
- An Ordinary Day in 2050
- The Green Invaders
- How Computers took over the World

- Students read out what they have written.

▶ **Language focus** (SB 31 TB 17)

● **Reading** (SB 25)

Students work in groups to prepare questions about Oscar Wilde and *The Picture of Dorian Gray*. This should serve as a good pre-reading task to provide information about the book, and to motivate students to want to read. Check that students' questions are well-formed. When they are ready, get students to ask you the questions. Don't worry if you don't know all the answers!

Here is some information to help you:

Oscar Wilde was born in Dublin in 1854, and died in Paris in 1900. He was a distinguished classical scholar at Dublin and Oxford, and was also a renowned poseur and wit. He believed in the central importance of art in life, which he considered should be lived with an aesthetic intensity. In London in the early 1880s, he established himself in social and artistic circles by his wit and flamboyance. In 1884 he married and had two children. He wrote poetry, reviews and plays, the most famous of which was *The Importance of Being Earnest*. *The Picture of Dorian Gray* was his only novel. He had a close friendship with Lord Alfred Douglas, whose father accused Wilde of being a homosexual. Wilde sued for criminal libel, but his case collapsed when the

evidence went against him, and he dropped the suit. Urged to flee to France by his friends, Wilde refused, unable to believe that his freedom was threatened. He was arrested and ordered to stand trial.

Wilde testified brilliantly, but the jury failed to reach a verdict. In the retrial he was found guilty and sentenced, in 1895, to two years' hard labour. He was released in 1897, a bankrupt, and went to France, where he died a few years later.

The Picture of Dorian Gray was published first in magazine form in 1890, and in book form in 1891. It combines elements of the Gothic novel with the unspeakable sins of decadent fiction. Critics accused the book of immorality. In reply, Wilde said 'There is no such thing as a moral or an immoral book. Books are well written or badly written.'
The main character is Dorian Gray, a very beautiful young man, who becomes vain, cruel and ever more decadent in the life he leads. However, the sins he indulges in are reflected in a portrait, which becomes more and more hideous (and which Dorian hides from view) and not in Dorian, who remains for ever young and beautiful.

- Read extracts 1 – 5 and answer the Comprehension check questions. If students have great problems with the vocabulary then explain some of it, but beware of stopping the flow (and the enjoyment) of the reading part of the lesson with too much vocabulary explanation. There is a glossary under each extract. Two vocabulary exercises follow the reading.

Rather than students reading silently, it can be very interesting at times for students to take it in turns to read aloud. This not only practises pronunciation, but it also means that the class is operating as a whole group and you can stop and discuss words and the text whenever you want.

Extract 1 (SB 25)

Comprehension check (SB 26)

Answers

1 *That he will lose his beauty as he grows older.*
2 *That the picture should grow old and that he should stay always young.*
3 *He appears to be terribly vain and naïve.*

Extract 2 (SB 26)

Comprehension check (SB 26)

Answers

4 *The expression on the face would appear to be changing. There are lines of cruelty around the mouth.*

5 *We don't really know at this stage. Although in reality such things are not possible, it is part of the suspension of disbelief on which this (horror) story is based that pictures can change appearance. At this point in the story, we don't know if it is Dorian's guilt that makes him see the change. Later, when the artist Hallward also sees the changed portrait, we can conclude that Dorian is not imagining it.*

Extract 3 (SB 26)

Comprehension check (SB 26)

Answers

6 *Whether to continue his life of passions and sins and let the portrait carry the burden for it, or whether to lead an honest life of propriety.*

7 *He is going to lead a life of passion, pleasure and sin. He would appear to be looking forward to the prospect of such self-indulgence and getting away with it.*

8 *It would show Dorian just how depraved he was becoming, and would reveal his mental state clearly.*

Extract 4 (SB 27)

Comprehension check (SB 27)

Answers

9 *To compare his physical beauty with the horrendous portrait. He gets a sense of pleasure from realizing that no one knows what he is doing.*

10 *He thinks that he is beautiful; he likes the idea that he is a corrupt person and that the picture shows him just how corrupt he is; and he wonders which parts of the portrait are more hideous, those parts that show the corruption of his soul or those which show him ageing.*

11 *He would appear to be losing his senses, becoming more and more irrational and out of touch with reality, and cut off from the rest of the world.*

Extract 5 (SB 27)

Comprehension check (SB 28)

Answers

12 *Because it was a physical reminder of all the sins he had committed. His attitude had changed because it no longer gave him the pleasure it used to. He would worry in case anyone else should see it.*

13 *To kill the past and to find peace of mind.*

14 *Presumably because either Sir Henry Ashton or his uncle had been badly treated by Dorian Gray at some time, and they relished anything unpleasant that might be happening in his household.*

15 *We have to guess a certain amount! Presumably Dorian tried to stab the canvas, but somehow or other the knife went through Dorian's heart, killing him. As a result, the portrait retained the physical beauty of the man, while the ugliness of his soul transferred to his body.*

Questions for discussion

Answers

1 *We don't know! Did his hand slip? Did the portrait make his hand slip? Dorian had sold his soul to the Devil – was it the Devil who was claiming a soul?*

3 *The original portrait had shown Dorian how physically beautiful he was, and the changing portrait would give him similar insights into his mind.*

4 *At the beginning he is rather young and simple. He was always in love with himself, but he becomes more cruel and calculating, finally taking leave of his senses.*

5 *People become richer emotionally and wiser as they grow old, but this is at the expense of the physical beauty of youth.*

Oscar Wilde's epigrams (SB 28)

– Read the epigrams together

> Much of his wit is based on paradox. For example, when he was asked his opinion of a play that was generally thought to have been a fiasco, he said, 'The play was a great success but the audience was a disaster.' He was asked to make certain changes in one of his plays. Wilde protested, 'Who am I to tamper with a masterpiece?' One version of his last words, as he was staying in a shabby Paris bedroom, is 'Either that wallpaper goes or I do.'

▶ **Language focus** (SB 31 TB 18)

● Vocabulary (1 SB 28)

1 Positive and negative meaning (SB 28)

– Students work in pairs to find the words with positive and negative meanings in lines 4-15, 78-99 and 148-55.

Answers

Lines 4 – 15
Positive
  delicate
Negative
  mar   dreadful   hideous   uncouth   pang

Lines 78 – 99
Positive
  fair   young   sensual   white
Negative
  evil   ageing   corruption   monstrous   seared wrinkling   coarse   bloated   misshapen   failing

Lines 148 – 55
Positive
 splendid   wonder   exquisite
Negative
 withered   wrinkled   loathsome

2 Dramatic style   (SB 28)

Answers

hideous – ugly
quiver – tremble
shuddering – shaking
to linger – to remain
flashed – came suddenly
infinite – endless
the verge – the edge
burdened – loaded down
melancholy – sadness
glistened – shone
seized – picked up
agony – pain
exquisite – beautiful, excellent

● Speaking and writing   (SB 29)

– The speaking acts as a prompt for writing.

Devising a horror story   (SB 29)

– Students work in groups of four to outline the plot of a horror story. This is an enjoyable activity that often produces some hilariously improbable stories. Don't underestimate the amount of time that students need to talk about their stories and then actually write them. Monitor the groups carefully and check their stories, correcting and explaining as necessary. After a time, perhaps 20-25 minutes, ask the groups to read out their stories, whether they are finished or not. Students write up the story for homework.

● Listening   (SB 30)

T.2

– Introduction: Have a short discussion on the subject of spy stories, asking questions such as the following:

Do you like spy stories?
Which authors do you like?
Do you find them easy to read?
Some spy stories are very complex. Why do you think an author makes a book hard to read?
Have you seen any spy films? What were they about?
Have you read any of Graham Greene's books, or seen any of the films of his books?

– Read the introduction to Graham Greene in the Student's Book.

– Students listen to the interview and take notes under the headings suggested.

Graham Greene speaks in a rather affected manner with an upper-class accent. He uses **one** and **one's** to refer to **me** and **my**. It might be of interest to your students to know that he suffered a nervous breakdown at the age of sixteen, and at the age of nineteen played Russian roulette several times for the thrill of it. He spent much of his life travelling to very dangerous parts of the world, working as a reporter covering wars and civil uprisings.

Answers

– *Graham Greene was seventy-eight at the time of the interview. He's tall and slim, and stoops. The interviewer describes him as modest and affable. Greene mentions that he had psychoanalysis when he was sixteen, perhaps because he was depressed. He talks about the boredom that he feels about life being like a disease. He has a sort of world-weariness, and an attitude that nothing in life is of any interest for more than an hour. This may be true or may be affected.*

– *He says an author must be cold, with no emotional involvement with a character.*

– *He quotes the examples of how he viewed the distress of a mother whose son had just died to get material for a book he was going to write.*

– *A minor character might be drawn from someone he knows, but the main character is imagined, a composite of all sorts of people including himself and his own experiences. He says that he hands over control of the narrative to the characters, although he knows the main direction of the plot. He even surprises himself sometimes that a story should have taken a certain direction.*

– *He says that a lot of his life is about trying to escape boredom, and even danger doesn't destroy boredom because after a while that too becomes boring.*

What do you think?   (SB 30)

– Answer the 'What do you think?' questions as a class.

● Vocabulary 2   (SB 30)

Words with the same spelling but different pronunciation   (SB 30)

1 The word minute /maɪnjuːt/ came up in the extracts from the *Picture of Dorian Gray*. Write the word on the board, and ask students if they know two meanings and two pronunciations for it.

– Read the introduction to the exercise.

- Students work in two groups to research their words, then explain them to the other group.

Answers

bow   /baʊ/ *You bow to the Queen.*
       /baʊ/ *A bow and arrow are used for hunting.*
tear   /teə/ *To tear your trousers on a nail.*
       /tɪə/ *A tear in her eye.*
row   /rəʊ/ *To row a boat.*
       /raʊ/ *To row means to have an argument.*
lead   /li:d/ *To lead a group or a march.*
       /led/ *Lead is a pliable, heavy grey metal.*
polish   /pɒlɪʃ/ *To polish your shoes.*
       /pəʊlɪʃ/ *Polish people live in Poland.*
used   /ju:st/ *I used to like ice-cream, but not any more.*
       /ju:zd/ *A used car, or I used a hammer to bang in the nail.*
live   /lɪv/ *Where do you live?*
       /laɪv/ *A live concert, or a live wire.*
wind   /wɪnd/ *The wind blows.*
       /waɪnd/ *To wind up a clock.*
wound   /waʊnd/ *I wound up the clock.*
       /wu:nd/ *A wound is a cut in your flesh.*
close   /kləʊz/ *To close a door.*
       /kləʊs/ *The post office is close to the bank.*

2 You could divide students up to do this question in a similar way to the previous question, so different groups are working on different words.

Answers

console   /kən'səʊl/ *To console someone who is unhappy.*
       /'kɒnsəʊl/ *A console is a panel with a lot of switches, for example, in a recording studio.*
entrance   /'entrəns/ *The entrance to a building.*
       /ɪn'trɑ:ns/ *If a performance entrances you, you feel delight and wonder.*
refuse   /rɪ'fju:z/ *To refuse to do something means to say no.*
       /'refju:s/ *Refuse is what dustmen collect.*
content   /kən'tent/ *Happy.*
       /'kɒntent/ *The contents page of a book.*
extract   /'ekstrækt/ *We read extracts from the Picture of Dorian Gray.*
       /ɪks'trækt/ *A dentist will extract a bad tooth.*
desert   /'dezət/ *The Sahara Desert.*
       /dɪ'zɜ:t/ *A soldier who deserts the army.*
contract   /'kɒntrækt/ *A legal contract.*
       /kən'trækt/ *To contract a disease, or metal contracts in the cold.*
object   /əb'dʒekt/ *To object to an idea or plan.*
       /'ɒbdʒekt/ *To have a large object in one's hand.*
incense   /'ɪnsens/ *Incense is burned in religious ceremonies.*
       /ɪn'sens/ *If you feel incensed, you are extremely angry.*
defect   /dɪ'fekt/ *A spy might defect to the enemy.*
       /'di:fekt/ *A defect is a fault or imperfection, for example, in someone's character.*
project   /'prɒdʒekt/ *A project is a plan.*
       /prə'dʒekt/ *The population of Britain is projected to rise slowly over the coming years. (= estimated)*
frequent   /'fri:kwənt/ *A frequent visitor comes often.*
       /frɪ'kwent/ *If you frequent a place, for example a bar, you go there often.*

LANGUAGE STUDY (SB 31)

T.3

1 Narrative tenses (1) (SB 31)

- Read the introduction to the exercise on narrative tenses (1) together.

- Students may want to read the Grammar Section before doing the exercise, especially the part on the future in the past.

> In this exercise, only two forms of the future in the past are tested, the Past Continuous and **would**. If students find this area difficult, try pointing out the absolutely logical connection between the future forms that they are familiar with (Present Continuous for arrangement, and **will** for intention and as auxiliary of the future) and their past equivalents.
> *Angus Pym will/would wake up on the dot of six . . .*
> *He is/was seeing M at nine o'clock this/that morning . . .*
> *He will/would have to pay more attention to his diet . . .*

- Students work in small groups to put the verbs in brackets in the correct tense. When the groups have finished, compare answers as a class to see if they agree, before playing the tape to check answers.

Answers

a. *woke*
b. *did*
c. *was*
d. *had been doing (had done is also possible. The continuous suggests the various activities he had been engaged in. The simple suggests the number of completed tasks.)*
e. *was still wearing*
f. *fell*
g. *came*
h. *had gone*
i. *had just finished*
j. *was looking (The Past Perfect Continuous isn't necessary here. The time aspect of past-in-the-past*

has already been established, and although logically speaking, questions j and k should be in the Past Perfect, too many examples of this tense, one after another, jar on the ear.)

  k. *was rudely interrupted*
  l. *thought (The simple suggests the completed action. It didn't take him five minutes to decide which suit to put on. The continuous would suggest that it took a long time, and that something else happened while he was thinking e.g. He was thinking about which suit to put on when the phone rang.)*
  m. *was seeing (an arrangement)*
  n. *wanted*
  o. *noticed*
  p. *had put (The continuous is just about possible.)*
  q. *would have to (The answer is **would** because it is like a reported thought. At the moment he saw himself in the mirror, Pym had the following spontaneous thought. 'I'll have to be more careful with my diet.'*
  r. *was driving/drove*
  s. *considered (The verb action implies duration, so the continuous isn't necessary here, although it wouldn't be wrong.)*
  t. *knew*
  u. *he had personally arranged*
  v. *controlled (The simple sounds better, but the continuous is just possible.*
  w. *would tell him (**would** for the same reason as q)*

▶ **Grammar reference:**   (SB 135)

2 Narrative tenses (2)   (SB 31)

– This shows how a writer uses tenses to look forwards and backwards.

– Read the explanation about narrative tenses (2) in the Language study section together.

> There is an extremely tense and dramatic ending to the book, as Dorian's mind races between the past-in-the-past (how the portrait had given him pleasure; how he had been worried that someone else might see it; how he had killed Hallward), the future-in-the-past (Was he going to confess? Would he destroy the portrait?) and the real past.

– Students work in pairs to comment on the use of tenses in lines 1–11 and lines 64–77. This is quite a challenging exercise, so give your students every encouragement, and don't worry about totally accurate answers. As long as they perceive past, past-in-the-past and future-in-the-past, that is enough. The aim of this exercise is **not** to have a long discussion about tense usage in subordinate clauses etc.!

Practice   (SB 31)

Answers

Lines 1 – 11
there would be a day Future-in-the-past – Dorian is predicting future events.
The scarlet would pass Ditto
The life that was to make Future-in-the-past. **Was to** has the meaning of **was destined to**.
would mar Future-in-the-past
He would become Ditto
As he thought Past Simple for real past time
a sharp pang of pain struck Ditto
made Ditto
deepened Ditto
came Ditto
felt Ditto
a hand of ice had been laid Past Perfect to express unreal past, which is dealt with in Units 7 and 11.

Lines 64 – 77
He felt Past Simple for real past time
the time had really come Past Perfect to express past-in-the-past
had his choice already been made Past Perfect (passive) to express past-in-the-past
life had decided Ditto
he was to have Future-in-the-past
portrait was to bear Ditto
that was all Past Simple for real past time
there would be Future-in-the-past
He would be able Ditto
portrait would be to him Ditto
it had revealed Past Perfect to express past-in-the-past
it would reveal Future-in-the-past
when winter came Future-in-the-past, but **would** is not used in subordinate clauses. There is no point in going into this area in any depth.
he would still be Future-in-the-past
where spring trembles Oscar Wilde has got his tenses mixed up! It should in fact be **trembled** for the same reason as *when winter came* above, but it just goes to show that this is quite a complex area, and one or two mistakes, as long as they are on the right lines, don't matter!

Lines 78 – 99
All the uses of **would** in this paragraph are to express past habit. Notice that **used to** is also used to express the same concept.

– There are further exercises on narrative tenses, the future-in-the-past, and **used to** versus **would** in Unit 2 of the Workbook.

3 Reflexive pronouns   (SB 31)

– Read the explanation about reflexive pronouns together.

Practice (SB 31)

1 Students work in pairs to compare the use or absence of pronouns.

Answers

a. *Get dressed does not usually require a reflexive pronoun, unless it is used to stress that this is a newly-acquired skill, for example for a child.*

b. *Burn/hurt/cut and other similar verbs (graze, injure etc.) require a reflexive when the part of the body involved is not specified. When it is specified, there is no reflexive.*

c. *By myself and on my own mean the same, that is, not with other people. I made it myself stresses that it was not bought.*

d. *The first sentence involves two people. In the second, only my wife is involved.*

e. *The first sentence is neutral. The second stresses the director. The third stresses the subject.*

f. *In the first sentence, the individual child looks after himself/herself. In the second, the action is reciprocal – each individual child looks after the other.*

2 Students work in pairs to discuss in what situations the sentences might be said.

Answers

a. *To a guest in your house.*

b. *To someone at the dinner table.*

c. *'Don't ask me to do it for you.'*

d. *This means 'Bring your emotions under control so that you behave calmly and reasonably.' It could be said to someone who is in an unreasonable panic.*

e. *'I forced myself to do it.'*

f. *This means 'I am annoyed with myself for being so stupid, or for missing an opportunity.' e.g. I could kick myself for messing up the exam. It was really easy.*

g. *This is like help yourself.*

h. *Myself means for me.*

i. *This is informal and rather rude. It means that you don't mind or care whether the person you're talking to does a particular thing or not. For example, 'Do you mind if I sit here?' 'Please yourself!'*

j. *A do-it-yourself shop is one that sells all you need to work on your home, for example, tools, wall-paper, paint etc.*

REVISION (SB 32)

– This focuses on irregular verbs to continue work on narrative tenses.

Irregular verbs (SB 32)

– Look at the dictionary entries and check that students understand the dictionary conventions to show Past Tense and Past Participle the same, Past Tense and Past Participle different, and spelling.

– Students work in pairs or small groups to see if they know the forms of the verbs. They could check their answers in a dictionary, but obviously not until they have done as many as they can together. This is a sort of memory test!

Take care with the following:

Hang is usually irregular (hang, hung, hung), except when it means to hang someone, when it is a regular verb. *He was hanged yesterday.*

Lay is transitive, which means it must have an object, for example, *to lay a table, a chicken lays eggs.* The Forms are lay, laid, laid.

Lie as in *not to tell the truth* is regular. The forms are lie, lied, lied.

Lie as in *to lie in bed* is irregular. The forms are lie, lay, lain.

Raise is transitive, for example, *to raise your hand, to raise children.* It is regular. The forms are raise, raised, raised.

Rise is intransitive, for example, *the sun rises, a cake rises.* It is irregular. The forms are rise, rose, risen.

Answers

2 *They can be both regular and irregular, with two spellings and two pronunciations, in British English.*
I burned/burnt the meal last night.
Have you learned/learnt the poem yet?
She spilled/spilt her coffee.
In American English, they are always regular.

With the **-t** spelling, the pronunciation is always /t/ at the end. For example:

dreamt /dremt/
learnt /lɜːnt/

With the **-ed** spelling, the pronunciation can be either /d/ or /t/ at the end.

burned /bɜːnd/ or /bɜːnt/
dreamed /driːmd/ or /dremt/
leaned /liːnd/ or /lent/
learned /lɜːnd/ or /lɜːnt/

When the participle is used as an adjective, the **-t** spelling is more usual.

burnt toast
spoilt child
spilt milk

3 Students work in pairs for five minutes, writing questions which will elicit the verbs in questions 1 and 2. Make sure the questions are well-formed.

EXTRA IDEAS

- The most obvious source of extra ideas for this unit will concern what students have read in the past, and what they are reading at the moment. There could be talks on students' previous reading, a writer they particularly like and admire, the novel that they remember best, the 'book versus the film' debate, famous writers from students' own countries, their literary traditions versus those in English/American literature, etc.

- This would be a good time to assign a class reader, if you haven't done so already, or to set up a class library. One interesting way of setting up the library is to take in a selection of books, and ask students (in pairs) to select one and look at every part of the book except the actual story. They study the jacket design, the blurb on the back, the biographical information about the author, previous publications, date of publication, etc., and on the basis of that decide what kind of book it is, what it might be about, and whether they would in fact want to read it. After a feedback session, students decide what they want to read.

- You could record an English speaking friend talking on one of the subjects outlined above or invite him/her to come into your class.

UNIT 3

What is normal?

OVERVIEW OF THE UNIT

– The theme of what is normal and abnormal behaviour for different people in different groups runs throughout the unit. This should provide opportunity for lots of discussion on topical issues relating to your particular students in your particular teaching situation. There is an article about a remarkable young man who lived in tree houses in Central Park, New York, a song by Noël Coward making fun of the British abroad, and an interview with Quentin Crisp, the writer and raconteur.

– There is a further exercise on synonyms in the second vocabulary section.

– The Revision section concentrates on future forms, which always present students with problems, in preparation for the language work on modal verbs in Unit 4.

NOTES ON THE LANGUAGE INPUT

'As' versus 'like'; constructions with 'as'

These areas do not present students with particular problems of concept, but there are problems of form. The various uses of **as** are examined, **as** is contrasted with **like**, and **as** is practised in various ways to express comparison.

Verb patterns

This is the first focus on verb patterns. This unit concentrates on verbs generally, while Unit 7 deals with verb patterns in reported speech. Most verbs present few conceptual problems – students simply have to remember which verbs are followed by an infinitive, which by an -ing form, and which need a preposition, etc. However, they often confuse those verbs which can take two different forms with a change in meaning, for example, **stop**, **remember**, **try**, **go on**, etc. These are

practised in the Student's Book and in more detail in the Workbook.

Future forms

Students have difficulty with all aspects of future forms, partly because there are so many in English, and partly because the form selected depends on how the speaker sees the event (aspect). At this level, you should be reminding students of the rules and the differences, rather than presenting them for the first time, but you can still anticipate some difficulties.

The most common forms are **will, going to** and the Present Continuous. The use of the Present Simple for the 'calendar' future is restricted and quite straightforward. The Future Perfect is also of low frequency, but the Future Continuous is worth drawing students' attention to in some depth. One of its uses is straightforward – like all continuous tenses, it expresses an activity in progress around a given time.

This time next week I'll be lying on the beach.

Its other use, to express an action that will happen naturally in the course of time, is more subtle.

So you've bought your new house? When will you be moving?

I'll be driving to London next week, so I'll give you a lift.

Draw students' attention to these two uses. Certainly the Future Continuous is used more than we might think. Try to pick up on examples that you come across in the course of your teaching.

NOTES ON THE UNIT

● **Discussion** (SB 33)

– Introduction: You could begin with the personalization exercise given at the end of this discussion, and ask students what groups they belong to at work, at home and in their free time. Ask questions such as the following:

What groups do you belong to?
What do you do in these groups?
Do you have to do things at certain times?
Are there any written or unwritten rules that have to be obeyed?

> If there isn't a lot of response at this stage, don't worry! You are asking students to step outside themselves and look at the groups they belong to quite objectively. It is important to stress that groups don't just mean formal organizations, but include such things as being a teenager, being a parent, being a smoker, being a vegetarian. By the time you come back to this topic at the end of the discussion, students should see more the kinds of things this unit is asking them to consider.

– Look at the cartoon and discuss the questions. (The joke hinges on us expecting to hear 'not wearing a club **tie**'. Notice how the key word **moustache** is the last word.)

– Students work in groups of four to discuss what is normal and abnormal behaviour for the groups of people listed. After a while, get their feedback and encourage cross-class discussion.

● Vocabulary 1   (SB 34)

1 Idioms   (SB 34)

– Students work in pairs to complete the idioms.

Answers

a. *fish*
b. *Romans*
c. *feather*
d. *himself*
e. *sore*
b and c refer to being the same as other people; a, d and e refer to being different.

– Ask students to translate similar idioms from their language.

2 Words with similar meaning   (SB 34)

– Students skim through the dictionary entries. The words all express something to do with being strange or odd.

– Using the dictionary entries, students work in pairs to correct the sentences.

Answers

a. *freak storm*
b. *eerie/weird voice*
c. *sounds really eerie*
d. *weird*
e. *fantastic design*
f. *uncanny*
g. *very eccentric*

3 Collocation   (SB 34)

– Students work in pairs to put the possible adjectives and nouns together. This exercise is quite difficult, as native speakers could well think certain collocations are or aren't possible. Only the common collocations are given in the answers.

Answers

weird/fantastic dream
weird/deviant/eccentric/idiosyncratic behaviour
freak accident
weird/eerie experience
weird/idiosyncratic style of painting
weird/eerie feeling
weird/eccentric person
weird/fantastic fashion
weird effect
eerie sound
weird/freakish appearance
weird/fantastic clothes
weird/eerie/fantastic place
Fantastic could be used with all nouns in its less literal meaning.

● Reading   (SB 35)

– Introduction: Ask students if they know of any eccentrics. Point out that eccentricity is often attractive in its strangeness rather than off-putting.

Pre-reading task   (SB 35)

Discuss the first question in the pre-reading task in pairs or small groups. The aim is prediction and motivation. Students should pick up on America being a land of opportunity and a land of dreams, and that a certain Mr Redman must have realized some kind of impossible dream. The writer says that there is a tirelessly competitive atmosphere in the United States.

Reading for information   (SB 35)

– Students read the article and answer the pre-set questions.

Answers

The dream that became a reality was Mr Redman finally being offered what for him is the perfect job – working with trees. There are three things that the writer seems to find comforting. Firstly, the happy ending of the story – Mr Redman wasn't put in jail, or locked up for being different; secondly, the way an eccentric can in fact find a place in society; and lastly, the fact that not all Americans are go-getting, competitive business people, but there are some gentler, nature-loving people.

Comprehension check/language work (SB 37)

– Students work in pairs to prepare the comprehension check/language work questions.

Answers

1 *Where do you get an extraordinary view of Central Park from? Or where does the writer suggest you should stay on your first visit to New York?*
2 *Who did people say lived in the treetops?*
3 *How long had Bob Redman been living in the trees?*
4 *How many tree houses did he build/had he built?*
5 *What does he like to do when he is in one of his tree houses?*
6 *What did he build the tree houses with?*
7 *How did he camouflage the tree houses?*
8 *How long did his final tree house last?*
9 *What did Mr Serpe find amazing/interesting/ marvellous about the last tree house?*
10 *What does the writer think of Mr Redman?*

Roleplay (SB 37)

– As a further comprehension check, and to provide some free speaking practice, students can work in pairs to act out the roleplay. The journalists could get together in one group and the 'Mr Redmans' in another group for five minutes to prepare what they are going to say, then pair up to conduct the roleplay. This has the advantage that students will then have more ideas about what to say or ask.

Vocabulary guessing (SB 37)

– You could briefly revise **would** for past habit by asking students to look at lines 75 – 92. There are three examples of **would**. Ask them what concept they express. They are all **would** for past habit.

▶ **Language focus** (SB 40 TB 24)

● Vocabulary 2 (SB 37)

| T.4 | **Introduction** (SB 37)

– Read the biographical information about Noël Coward.

Clipped speech is talking in quick, short sounds that are not joined together. It is typical of an upper-class accent.

Questions to discuss before you listen (SB 37)

– Discuss these questions as a class.

Answers (*Answers to question 4*)
a – 7   c – 2   e – 6   g – 3
b – 5   d – 1   f – 4

Listening and vocabulary (SB 38)

– Read the introduction. Students look at the first verse and try to fill the gaps with one of the words in the right hand column. They should consult their dictionaries if necessary and discuss which pair fits where and which word of each pair is most suitable.

– Play the first verse so that students can check their answers.

Notice that in line 7 of the first verse, Coward changes **ultra** to **ultry** (a word which doesn't exist) to fit the rhyme with sultry.

● Discussion (SB 39)

Culture shock! (SB 39)

– Choose how best the questions should be answered. For multi-lingual groups, one possibility would be for students to discuss the first two questions in groups, then as a class exchange feedback, and finally discuss the last two questions as a class. For monolingual groups (especially those in their own country and who have not travelled) concentrate on questions 3 and 4 in groups and as a class.

Writing (SB 39)

– We recommend that you first do the exercise on linking cause and result on page 21 of the Workbook.

– Students write their essays for homework.

● Listening (SB 40)

| T.5 |

– Introduction: Tell your students a little about Quentin Crisp.

Quentin Crisp was born in 1908, and realized at a very early age that he was homosexual. He was very close to his mother, but his father disapproved of him terribly. Realizing that he was outside what was considered the norm, he had to decide whether to hide it or show it to the world, and he chose the second. He began wearing eye make-up and lipstick in public in the 1930s when it was even quite shocking for women to do this. Naturally, he was ridiculed, scorned and attacked, but his defence was indifference and witty retorts. All his life he revelled in his sloth – he did as little as possible, worked only when forced to, mainly as a life model for painters. He boasts in his autobiography, as he mentions in the interview, that he never cleaned any room that he lived in. 'After three years,' he says, 'it doesn't get any dirtier.' When he was 21, he went to live in America, where he now lives permanently. When speaking, he has certain idiosyncrasies. He has a very nasal voice, and draws words out slowly, but his timing for witty remarks is very clever. Towards the end of the interview, he says 'Otherwise and that' twice, when usually we would just say 'Otherwise' – it is part of his way of speaking.

– Read the introduction to the interview as a class.
– Students listen to the interview and answer the questions.

Comprehension check   (SB 40)

Answers

1 *That he would never be like other people, and he couldn't pretend that he was.*
2 *To a certain extent, they are just like everyone else in the world, part of the human race that he wasn't part of. He talks about them indifferently, showing no surprise that they laughed at him just the same as everyone else did. Later he says that he got to know his mother well, when they were both older.*
3 *Someone who doesn't conform to society in every way.*
4 *They were obviously shocked and surprised by the way he dressed and presented himself. His mother seems to have accepted him more than his father.*
5 *One large room where everything he wanted to do could easily be done.*
6 *On the one hand, he would appear to enjoy being an eccentric, flamboyant, larger-than-life character, capable of dealing with the scorn directed at him with wit and charm, but on the other hand, there is a profound sadness that he should have felt an outsider all his life.*

▶ **Language focus**   (SB 41 TB 24–5)

LANGUAGE STUDY   (SB 40)

1 'As'

– Students re-read the text about Mr Redman to find the seven examples of **as** or **as . . . as**.

Answers

35 *regarded as* **As** used after certain verbs
52 *as birds build nests* **As** for comparisons
67 *describe as* **As** after certain verbs
72 *as well as* **As** + adjective/adverb + **as** construction
83 *as many as* **As** + adjective/adverb + **as** construction
96 *as long as* **As** + adjective/adverb + **as** construction
121 *As the officers* **As** = while

'As' versus 'like'   (SB 40)

– Read the examples. Students try to answer the questions and work out the rules.

Answers

The second and third sentences are comparisons.
Like a monkey is **like** + *a noun.*
As birds build nests is **as** + *a clause.*
In the first and last sentence, **as** *means in the manner of.*

▶ **Grammar reference:**   (SB 136)

– Students read the Grammar section for homework, or in class as it is not very long.

Practice   (SB 40)

– Students work in pairs to complete the sentences with **as** or **like**.

Answers

a. *like*
b. *as . . . like*
c. *as . . . as*
d. *as . . . like*
e. *like . . . as*

'As . . . as' for comparison   (SB 40)

Answers

1 a. *Alan doesn't enjoy his work as much as she does.*
  b. *I've never been as happy as I am today!*
  c. *He isn't as interesting to talk to as he used to be.*
  d. *His later books aren't as appealing as his earlier ones.*
  e. *Alice doesn't speak German as well as I do.*
  f. *She isn't as arrogant as I thought.*

2 a. *many*
  b. *much*
  c. *well*
  d. *long*
  e. *soon*
  f. *far*

– There are several exercises in the Workbook that practise **as . . . as** for comparisons.

2 Verb Patterns   (SB 41)

– Students work in pairs to decide which of the verb forms fits the pattern, and what has to change to make the other verb forms fit.

Answers

a. **used** is the form that fits.
   Corrections
   He enjoys living . . .
   He is used to living . . .
   He would rather live . . .

b. **have decided** is the form that fits.
   Corrections
   I am thinking of looking . . .
   I had better look . . .
   I made him look . . .
c. **don't mind** is the form that fits.
   Corrections
   I was made to clean . . .
   I expect you to clean . . .
   I am trying to clean . . .
d. **want** is the form that fits.
   Corrections
   I stopped him from going.
   I hoped that he would go.
   I let him go.
e. **reminded him** is the form that fits.
   Corrections
   I remember him coming . . .
   I succeeded in coming . . .
   I am looking forward to coming . . .
f. **avoided** is the form that fits.
   Corrections
   I managed to meet him.
   I happened to meet him.
   I helped her (to) meet him.
g. **stopped** is the form that fits.
   Corrections
   I can't help doing it.
   I don't feel like doing it.
   I saw him do/doing it. (The infinitive suggests I
   saw him do the complete action; the -ing form
   suggests I saw him in the act of doing it.)

– In the Workbook, there are further exercises on verb
   forms, including verbs that take both infinitive and
   -ing with a change in meaning (**used; forget; stop;
   remember** etc.), and infinitive or **-ing** form after
   verbs of perception.

REVISION   (SB 41)

– This prepares students for the language work on
   modal verbs in Unit 4.

Future forms   (SB 41)

▶ **Grammar reference:**   (SB 136)

– Ask students to read the Grammar section for
   homework before doing this revision.

– Students work in pairs or small groups to match
   future forms to the correct definition.

Answers

1   a – 6   c – 3   e – 2   g – 1   i – 8
    b – 4   d – 7   f – 5   h – 9

2   *The Present Continuous e*
    The Future Continuous g, h
    Will + infinitive a, b
    The Present Simple f
    Going to + infinitive c, d
    The Future Perfect i

3   Students should read through each dialogue to
    understand the context before attempting the answer.

    a. *What are you doing/are you going to do*
    b. *We're going/going to go*
    c. *We're staying/going to stay*
    d. *won't be/isn't*
    c. *We'll probably/We probably won't come*
    f. *we're going to do*
    g. *We're going to visit/visiting*
    h. *we'll be lying*
    i. *How long will you be/are you going to be/are you
       away for?*
    j. *term starts*
    k. *we'll be back*
    l. *How long are you going to stay/are you staying*
    m. *what are you going to do/are you doing*
    n. *I'm going/going to go*
    o. *my English will have improved*
    p. *what will you do/are you going to do?*
    q. *I'll have to see*
    r. *I'm going/I'm going to go/I'll be going*
    s. *What are you going to do/are you doing/will you
       be doing*
    t. *I'm meeting/I'm going to meet*
    u. *How are you going to do/will you do*
    v. *I'll have sold*
    w. *you'll be making*
    x. *What are you going to do/will you do*
    y. *I'll let*

4   **Situation and characters**

Student C is called **Alex Manning**, and is going on a
short business trip to New York for his/her company.
Student A is **a colleague**, who is going to ask questions
about the trip.
Student D is called **Pat Kelly**, and is the United States
representative for the same company. He/she has
organized Alex's trip.
Student B is **Pat's boss** in America, and is going to check
with Pat that all the arrangements have been made.
Note that the names Alex and Pat have been chosen
because they can be both male or female names.

Stages of the roleplay

– The roleplay is in three stages.

1   All students are in four different groups, preparing
    their role from their rolecard.

2   Alex Manning (Student C) talks to a colleague
    (Student A) about the trip, while Pat Kelly (Student
    D) talks to his/her boss (Student B) to make sure that
    trip has been arranged.

3 Just one Alex Manning talks to one Pat Kelly over the phone (with the rest of the class listening) to finalize the arrangements. The reason for this is as follows. The information that Alex has is slightly different from the information that Pat has, and this will come out as they talk. (If *all* the students who are Alex and *all* the students who are Pat talked to each other, that would leave the colleagues and the bosses with no one to talk to. Besides, students will have done the bulk of the activity by this stage, and to conclude it concisely is more satisfying than stretching out an activity until everyone is fed up with it.)

Procedure for the roleplay

– Photocopy the rolecards on the next page. Allocate the roles A, B, C, D evenly to students. If the number of students in your class does not divide by four, additional A, B or C roles can be allocated. This will mean that one A, B or C role is shared by two students.

  Give out the rolecards and let students prepare together in their groups. (All role As together, all Bs together, etc.) Allow up to five minutes, or until students feel ready.

– Ask the students to pair up as follows to conduct the roleplay. One from Group A (colleague) with one from Group C (Alex Manning). One from Group B (boss) with one from Group D (Pat Kelly).

  Monitor students carefully to see how they are getting on, and when they have finished.

– Stop the roleplay, and say 'Now Alex is going to phone Pat in New York to make sure that all the arrangements are all right. Remember that the information that Alex has is provisional. Pat has the final arrangements, so there might be some changes.'

– Appoint *one* Alex and *one* Pat. Prompt Alex to start the conversation, for example, by saying 'Pat, hello! This is Alex Manning from London. I was just ringing . . . ' It would be useful to tape record this conversation so that afterwards the class can examine it for the use of future forms.

– There are four differences in the information they both have, and these should come out. First, Alex's plane arrives at Newark Airport, not John F Kennedy; next, Pat won't be there to meet him/her, he/she has to get a taxi; then on Thursday afternoon they are driving to Washington DC to inspect a new machine and staying overnight; and finally, the plane home leaves at 8.15 in the morning, not 9.15.

– Students could have similar conversations about their plans for this evening, this weekend, their next holidays, etc.

EXTRA IDEAS

– Find some current newspaper articles which deal with the case of any minority groups, for example, ethnic minorities, homosexuals, pressure groups such as Greenpeace, Friends of the Earth, Animal Liberation Front etc., and examine to what extent the newspaper deals with the subject fairly and without bias. If you are teaching outside Britain, these articles could be in the students' own language and the activity would work just as well, giving you the opportunity to discuss localized issues. The activity could also be enhanced if you can find two or more different newspaper treatments of the same topic, and thus explore the bias of liberal and popular press.

– Speaking activities will come from the suggestions above. There could also be discussions on the various -isms, sexism, racism, and ageism, prejudice against poor people, children, the handicapped, and perhaps on a more light-hearted note, left-handed people.

– Following the roleplay or in a subsequent lesson, practice in future forms can be developed in a free activity based on students' own future plans. Ask them to work in groups of two or three and ask each other about their plans for this evening, the weekend, after the course, further studies, a career. Afterwards, questioners can report their colleagues' most interesting or unusual plans to the class. The teacher should monitor the correct use of future forms and discuss students' uncertainties.

ROLE CARDS

Role A   A colleague of Alex Manning

You work for the same company as Alex Manning, based in London. Today is Monday. On Wednesday, Alex is going away on a short business trip.

Prepare to ask him/her questions about the trip.

Where . . .?
How long . . . ?
. . . flying from?
How long . . . flight?
Which airline . . . ?
. . . meeting you?
. . . staying?
. . . Wednesday evening?
. . . sight seeing?
. . . coming back?

Role B   Pat Kelly's boss

You work for a multi-national company (based in London) in their New York office. One of your staff is called Pat Kelly, a representative. You are his/her boss.

Today is Monday. On Wednesday, an English colleague of yours, Alex Manning, is coming out from London to New York for a few days. Pat Kelly has planned the trip.

You want to make sure that all the arrangements have been made satisfactorily, so you are going to talk to Pat Kelly.

Prepare to ask questions about the trip.

When . . . arrive?
Which airport . . . ?
How long . . . flight?
Which airline . . . ?
How many days . . . ?
. . . staying?
How . . . from the airport to the hotel?
. . . Wednesday evening?
. . . Thursday?
. . . Friday?
. . . going back?

Role C   Alex Manning

Your name is Alex Manning.
You work for a multi-national company based in London.

Today is Monday. On Wednesday you're going on a business trip to New York. The trip has been organized by Pat Kelly, your company's representative in New York.

Below is some provisional information about the trip. A colleague of yours is going to ask you about it.

Depart Wednesday 11.00 am, Heathrow terminal 4
British Airways BA 112 to John F Kennedy
Arrive New York 12.00 midday local time
Flight time is about 7 hours

Accommodation
Hotel La Plaza, 42nd Street

Schedule
Wednesday
12.00   Pat Kelly will meet you and take you to your hotel
7.00   Cocktail party at the Continental Hotel
8.30   Supper at Pat's home

Thursday
9.00   Trade fair all morning
2.00   Meeting clients all afternoon
6.00   Evening free – sight-seeing? Look up some friends?

Friday
9.00   Tour round new offices in New York in the morning
1.00   Meet new sales staff over lunch
3.00   Rest of day free

Saturday   *Return home*
Depart 9.15 am John F Kennedy
British Airways BA 332 to Heathrow
Arrive Heathrow 7.00 pm local time

Role D   Pat Kelly

Your name is Pat Kelly.
You are the United States representative for a multi-national company based in London. You are in New York.

Today is Monday. On Wednesday, an English colleague of yours, Alex Manning, is coming out from London to New York for a few days. You have planned the trip and sent him/her a copy of the schedule. Since then, a few things have changed.

Here is the final schedule. Your boss is going to talk to you to check that all the arrangements have been made.

Schedule for Alex Manning
Depart Wednesday 11.00 am, Heathrow terminal 4
British Airways BA 112 to Newark Airport
Arrive New York 12.00 midday New York time
Flight time is about 7 hours

Accommodation
Hotel La Plaza, 42nd Street

Wednesday
12.00   Alex gets taxi to the hotel. (Pat was going to meet Alex but this is no longer possible)
7.00   Cocktail party at the Continental Hotel
8.30   Supper at Pat's house

Thursday
9.00   Trade fair all morning
2.00   Drive to Washington DC to inspect a new machine, and stay overnight

Friday
9.00   Drive back to New York
1.00   Meet sales staff in new office over lunch
3.00   Rest of the day free

Saturday   *Return home*
Depart 8.15 am John F Kennedy
British Airways BA 332 to Heathrow
Arrive Heathrow 6.00 pm London time

NOTE: you may make photocopies of these cards for classroom use (but please note that copyright law does not normally permit multiple copying of published material).

UNIT 4

From the cradle to the grave

OVERVIEW OF THE UNIT

- A theme of people at different ages runs throughout the unit, beginning with the relationship between parent and child, then a look at bringing up children, and finally a humorous talk by the American comedian, George Burns, on how to live to be a hundred.
- The language work in this unit focuses on modal auxiliary verbs, which are a very rich and subtle area of English.

NOTES ON THE LANGUAGE INPUT

Modal auxiliary verbs

- Students will be familiar with many of the concepts that modal auxiliary verbs express, but by no means all of them, as they are quite a remarkable area of the language, and whole books have been written about them! The unit concentrates on modal verbs to express probability and modal verbs in their present and past forms.

- Students will probably know **must/can't, may, might** and **could** to express probability, but not **will** and **should**. Don't worry too much about the differences between **will, must/can't** and **should**, as they are very subtle and hard to explain clearly. It is probably enough that students recognize the different uses, and settle for more familiar forms in production. Students often avoid using **may/might/could** to express probability by using **will perhaps**, so try to encourage these forms. Notice that although **might** can be seen as the past form of **may**, and hence it expresses less likelihood, many speakers see no difference between the two forms.

NOTES ON THE UNIT

● Discussion   (SB 43)

T.6

Introduction: Ask students to tell the class either about their own children or about their young nephews, nieces and cousins.

- *What do they like doing?*
  What are their favourite toys and games?
  What games do they play with their friends and with you?
  Are they well-behaved?

- Discuss the first three questions as a class.

- Students work in small groups to answer question 4. They could argue for several possibilities as long as there is a logical link between the two halves.

Answers

If a child lives with criticism, she learns to condemn.
If a child lives with hostility, he learns to fight.
If a child lives with ridicule, she learns to be shy.
If a child lives with shame, he learns to feel guilt.
If a child lives with tolerance, she learns to be patient.
If a child lives with encouragement, he learns confidence.
If a child lives with praise, she learns to have faith.
(These last two could be reversed, as they express similar ideas.)
If a child lives with fairness, he learns justice.
If a child lives with security, she learns to appreciate.
If a child lives with approval, he learns to like himself.
If a child lives with acceptance and friendship, he or she learns to find love in the world.

- Students work in small groups to answer question 5. Ask one student in each group to take some notes. After five minutes, get class feedback.

Listening (SB 45)

– Stop the tape after each person has spoken and encourage discussion.

Answers

1 *The woman was encouraged and praised, and so learned confidence and faith.*

2 *The man wasn't encouraged as a child, his father ridiculed him and perhaps made him feel ashamed. It sounds as if he wasn't approved of for what he was, either. In later life, he might feel insecure, withdrawn and unwilling or unable to express himself openly.*

3 *The man's parents sound as though they were tolerant and friendly, and also perhaps encouraging and fair! As a result, he grew up to be a well-balanced, open, welcoming sort of person.*

4 *The man didn't seem to have his parents' friendship, and as they gave so little time to him, he wasn't encouraged or approved of. Hence perhaps he turned to drugs for the company of other drug-takers.*

5 *The girl obviously did not have a very secure childhood, and might find relationships with the opposite sex difficult, as there had been several father figures in her life but no solid relationship with her natural father.*

6 *The woman had a secure relationship with her mother, who treated her children fairly. As a result, she probably has a good relationship with her mother in later life.*

● Vocabulary 1 (SB 45)

1 Word building (SB 45)

– Students work in pairs to put a suitable word into each gap.

Answers

a. *condemned*

b. *hostile, unfair, discouraging (not **critical** next to **critics** for reasons of style)*

c. *justifiable (**tolerable** + **acceptable** do not collocate with **theft**)*

d. *fair (**just** does not collocate with **deal**)*

e. *intolerable*

f. *intolerant, critical, disapproving (not **impatient**, which takes **with**)*

g. *disapprovingly*

h. *unacceptable*

i. *appreciative*

j. *discourage*

2 Prepositions (SB 45)

Answers

a. *about; of*
b. *to; in*
c. *about; for; of*
d. *with; of*

e. *with; in*
f. *of; of*
g. *to; to*
h. *in; of*

– Remember there are additional exercises on prepositions in every odd-numbered unit of the Workbook.

● Reading (SB 45)

| T.7 | **Background information** (SB 45) |

– Students divide into two groups. Group A listens to the short talk given by Dr Spock, and Group B reads the letter written to a newspaper. Having discussed their answers in groups, they then pair up with a member from the other group to swap information.

> The two texts put forward different views on childhood and parenthood, and the world that children are growing up into. The dates of the texts are interesting. Spock was speaking in 1973, the year the Vietnam war ended, and is very optimistic in tone. He saw huge improvements in the way parents dealt with their children, and hoped that the spirit of free thinking would produce a happy, peaceful and reasonable generation. The letter was written in the more caustic 1980s, and is bitter and pessimistic in tone. Youth, he says, has learned to question too much, and is less concerned with other people and totally concerned with individual happiness. Pressures on children drive them to mental illness and drug abuse. There are sufficient issues raised for your class to discuss any or all of them.

Pre-reading task (SB 46)

– Introduction: Ask students if they know what a greenhouse is, and tell them that another word for greenhouse is hothouse. Explain that some American parents are so keen for their children to succeed in life that they are hothousing them. Ask if they can work out what this means. (It means the kind of things that the magazine article describes – trying to teach children to be superchildren.)

– Answer the two questions as a class.

Reading for information

– Students read the article, underlining anything that surprises them, and any flaws in Glenn Doman's thinking.

Answers

There can be no set answer, obviously. One has to wonder whether every child has the potential to be a genius. Do parents do these things to improve the child or to satisfy themselves? There seems to be an element of trying to impress the neighbours. Doman presumably has a scientific background, but it is a little suspicious that he refuses to prove his claims to other scientists.

Comprehension check   (SB 46)

Answers

1 *True*	6 *False*	9 *False*
2 *False*	7 *False*	10 *False*
3 *False*	8 *False* (The article	
4 *True*	doesn't exactly say it	
5 *False*	is a full-time job.)	

– Ask students about the tone of the article, and what the writer's attitude is towards the content.

> The writer seems to mock gently. The first paragraph sounds like an advertisement for washing powder; no doubt the most sensational cardinal facts have been selected; there is a sardonic reference to Shakespeare's Seven Ages of Man speech in *As You Like It*, where the infant is referred to as mewling and puking (crying and being sick) in the nurse's arms – the child that cries and vomits isn't just a child but a genius; the mothers are described rather sarcastically.

Points for discussion   (SB 48)

– Discuss these questions as a class. Some points will be relevant to the written homework below.

▶ **Language focus**   (SB 50, TB 31)

● Speaking   (SB 48)

Roleplay   (SB 48)

– Students work in pairs to write questions to put to Glenn Doman.

– They put their questions either to you or another member of the class.

● Writing   (SB 48)

– Do the exercise on **linking devices of similarity and comparison** on page 28 of the Workbook.

– Students choose one of the topics, and write about it for homework. You could ask students to choose in class, and they could pool ideas in groups during class time.

● Listening   (SB 48)

T.8

How to live to be a hundred or more

– Tell the following joke.

A man who lived to be a hundred was asked the secret of his long life.

'Don't smoke, don't drink, and get lots of sleep.'

'But,' said the interviewer, 'I knew someone who didn't smoke, didn't drink and got lots of sleep, and he died when he was 70!'

'Ah, well,' came the reply, 'He didn't keep it up long enough, did he!'

– Ask students in pairs to write down ten things they should or shouldn't do if they want to live to be a hundred. Encourage them to think of humourous things as well as the more serious matters to do with health care. After a while, ask for feedback.

Introduction   (SB 48)

– Read the introduction as a class.

Note-taking   (SB 48)

– Students listen to the extracts from George Burns's book *How to live to be a hundred or more*. (These are read by an actor, but his voice sounds very like that of George Burns.) They take notes and then compare in pairs. You could listen in sections for this activity.

Listening for specific points   (SB 48)

– Students listen again, perhaps reading the tapescript as well, to find the ways in which he tries to be funny.

● Vocabulary 2   (SB 49)
Euphemisms   (SB 49)

– Read the introduction as a class. Students work in pairs to put the correct euphemism into each gap.

Answers

1 – *g*
2 – *j*
3 – *m*
4 – *b* (An allotment is a small area of land rented in a town for people to grow things, usually vegetables.)
5 – *c*
6 – *a/o*
7 – *a/o*
8 – *h* (A work-to-rule is a form of protest in a job, where all the rules are followed exactly, but no one does any of the extra work which usually makes things go smoothly. The result is that people work more slowly, and less work is done.)
9 – *k*
10 – *n*
11 – *l*
12 – *d*
13 – *i*
14 – *e*
15 – *p*
16 – *f*

– Look at the other examples of euphemisms, and work out what they mean.

Answers

The rebels were killed.
The Prime Minister lied.
Your figures are wrong.
Could you pay off your overdraft?
We had an argument.
This is a risky policy.
The company is making a loss.

– You could show students an extract from *The Principles of Newspeak* at the back of George Orwell's *1984*, where he explores further euphemisms.

LANGUAGE STUDY   (SB 50)

1 Modal auxiliary verbs, present and future   (SB 50)

– Ask students to read the Grammar Section on modal auxiliary verbs as homework before you begin this lesson.

– Read the introduction. Ask students which modal verb expresses the strongest probability (**will**) and which expresses the weakest (**might** and **could**).

▶ **Grammar reference:**   (SB 137)

Practice   (SB 50)

– Students work in small groups to answer the questions. Be as encouraging as you can, as the exercises are quite difficult.

Answers

1 *Degrees of likelihood are expressed in sentences b, d, g, h, j, k, m, n and p.*
2 *Certainty – will, won't (d, g, h)*
  Probability – must, can't, should (b, m, p)
  Possibility – may, might, could (j, k, n)
3 *Obligation – must, mustn't, should (l, o)*
  Permission – can, may (a, i)
  Ability – can, can't (c)
  Willingness – will, won't (e, f)

2 Modal auxiliary verbs in the past   (SB 50)

▶ **Grammar reference:**   (SB 138)

Answers

a. *She could ski*
b. *I was able/managed to finish*
c. *Shakespeare can't/couldn't have lived*
d. *I was allowed to leave*

e. *I had to check*
f. *It must have been raining*
g. *You needn't have given*
h. *He didn't need to collect*
i. *You might have passed*
j. *He should have stopped*
k. *I could have visited*
l. *It will have been*
m. *He would sit*
n. *They may have got lost*

Practice   (SB 50)

3 Modal auxiliary verbs: past, present, and future   (SB 51)

Answers

a. *I don't have to*
b. *I might*
c. *the children must be*
d. *I'll have to*
e. *They won't*
f. *I should get up*
g. *they might wreck*
h. *they might not be/ can't be*
i. *I should have put out*
j. *I really must get up*
k. *dog must have hidden*
l. *We should have trained/ should train*
m. *we didn't have/need to*
n. *Alan might be*
o. *Why won't he take*
p. *We could have got*

– There are exercises in the Workbook on modal auxiliary verbs to express probability, possibility, ability, obligation, and **will** and **would** to express characteristic behaviour.

REVISION   (SB 51)

T.9

Reply questions

– Students listen to the short conversation. The man shows interest by using reply questions.

– Students try to remember the lines of the conversation. You could play it again for them. Make sure their intonation rises on the reply questions.

– Read the explanation of reply questions.

3 Students work in pairs to underline the correct auxiliary verb. This question tests them on **have** as a full verb versus **have** as an auxiliary verb in perfect tense versus **have** as a modal auxiliary to express obligation, and whether the contraction **'d** is short for **had** or **would**.

Answers

a. *Do you?* (**Have** here is a full verb referring to an activity.)
b. *Haven't you?* (**Have** is an auxiliary verb.)
c. *Has/does she?* (Both are possible. **Have** is a full verb referring to a state.)

d. *Did you?* (**Have** is a full verb in the Past Simple. The negative would be *I didn't have*, not **I hadn't.*)

e. *Do you?* (**Have** is used as a modal auxiliary verb to express obligation.)

f. *Had he?* (**Had** is an auxiliary verb used to form the Past Perfect.)

g. *Would he?* (**Would** expresses either willingness, or a suppressed second conditional – *he would help you if you asked him.*)

4 **Sample answers**

a. *Has he? What's he got?*

b. *Have you? When did that start?*

c. *Do you? Are you sure you've got the right mattress?*

d. *Did you? What was it about?*

e. *Didn't you? That's awful!*

f. *Would you? Poor you!*

g. *Had they? Why did you get there so late?* or *How embarrassing!* (You could discuss cultural differences regarding party-going here.)

h. *Doesn't he? How does he manage that?*

i. *Does he? That's incredible!*

j. *Doesn't he? That's not fair!*

5 Students work in pairs to do the roleplay.

– There is an exercise on page 27 of the Workbook which practises various question tags and reply questions.

EXTRA IDEAS

– Interview English-speaking friends on the subject of their childhood, where they grew up, their attitudes to brothers, sisters, grandparents and parents.

– Select topics for discussion from the following:

– Compare the childhood of your grandparents, parents and your own, in terms of education, entertainment, travel, duties, discipline, etc.

– Would you like to bring up your children in the same way that your parents brought you up?

– With a multinational class, you could try to discover differences in attitudes to bringing up children in the countries represented in class.

– For another possible thread to this unit, see the supplementary reading text on this page. Look at the Seven Ages of Man speech in Shakespeare's *As You Like It*, Act II, Scene 7, (*Headway Upper Intermediate* Student's Book, page 11) and compare it with the seven ages of man as described in Fritz Spiegl's *Keep Taking the Tabloids!* This could lead to an interesting examination of popular newspapers and their treatment of human interest stories. Ask students to buy a popular English newspaper and dissect it to see the kinds of stories in it – how much is foreign news, politics, comment, gossip, home news, entertainment and human interest?

The Fleet Street ages of man

The Ages of Man as seen by Fleet Street may begin with a 'miracle baby', which becomes a 'babe-in-arms', grows into a 'toddler', 'tot' and then a 'kid'. If his parents are divorced and disputing custody, he may turn into a 'tug-of-love' baby, toddler, or kid – with horrific suggestions of two people tearing out his arms as in a tug-of-war. Schoolchildren are sometimes described as school 'students', especially in the left-wing and sociological press while still 'teenagers'. Girl teenagers who become pregnant are 'gymslip mums' when they are still are school, but mere 'mums-to-be' as soon as they have left, even at the age of fifteen and still wearing their gymslips. An illegitimate baby is a 'love-child', and the place in which it is thought to have been produced, a 'love-nest' – for love is apparently thought never to enter into married relationships. A 'boy' becomes a 'youth' at about sixteen and a man at nineteen; but he may remain a 'boy-friend' even into his seventies. Women can be called 'girls' into their mid-thirties and 'girl-friends' up to any age. When actors, actresses or ballet dancers are the subject of a story they remain 'boys' and 'girls' for ever. There are also compound terms which can be made into almost any permutation, such as 'teenage fathers', 'gymslip muggers' or 'singing bachelor' etc. The subject's marital or professional status ('bachelor', 'businessman', 'housewife', 'divorcee'), his or her age, whether germane to the story or not – and, if a woman, her hair colour, breast, waist and hip measurements and some indication of her attractiveness, with carefully graded euphemisms ('blonde, vivacious have-a-go housewife, Eileen Grunge, 38, 44, 49') – are considered essential information. So are the existence and number of children, if any; and even the knowledge that the subject's children have proved their own fertility ('battling grandfather of four, Bert Snodgrass, 73'). But from the age of sixty to sixty-five Fleet Street Man's decline is rapid – into plain pensioner, sans teeth, sans dignity, sans everything.

Fritz Spiegl *Keep taking the tabloids!*

UNIT 5

War and peace

OVERVIEW OF THE UNIT

– The theme of war runs throughout the unit. We have tried to adopt a liberal, objective attitude to the subject, and although it can fascinate, it can also repel, so you need to exercise a large amount of caution in the way you approach this unit.
There is an article on the origins of war, and an interview with various soldiers who were present at the 1914 Christmas truce.

NOTES ON THE LANGUAGE INPUT

Ways of adding emphasis

This area presents students with no problems of concept, and very few of form, but you do need to make sure that they sound emphatic! Students will no doubt have come across ways of adding emphasis in their reading and listening before, but perhaps not had these formally presented before. This is the first focus on this area; it is picked up on again in Unit 10 and Unit 12.

Review of tenses

This deals with tenses generally, but with many examples of the passive. The perfect aspect is reviewed in the Revision section. The Past Perfect was dealt with in Unit 2 and the Future Perfect in Unit 3. This section aims to bring together the features that all perfect tenses have in common, and to give students some extra practice in the Present Perfect, one of the most difficult tenses for students to get right. This is because, although the same form exists in many other European languages, its use in English is different. There are three main uses of the Present Perfect.

(i) To express unfinished past.
I've lived here all my life.
He's been working with us for the past five years.

(ii) To express experience.
Have you ever seen the Queen?
Have you ever been travelling on the underground when all the lights went out?
It's the first time I've been here.

(iii) To express present interest in past events.
I've lost my passport.
What have you been doing since I last saw you?

NOTES ON THE UNIT

● Discussion   (SB 52)

– Introduction: Ask students on their own to write a definition of war. Write on the board 'War is . . .', and give them a minute or so, then get their definitions. You could tell them the depressing piece of graffiti 'Peace is the period of time between wars'.

– Students work in groups of three to match a quotation with its source. Your students may know some of them, or they might use a process of elimination.

Sources   (SB 53)

Answers

1 *Julius Caesar, at the end of the Pontic campaign, battle of Zela AD 47. (Zela is now called Zile and is located near Amasya, Turkey.)*
2 *US veteran of Vietnam*
3 *Recruiting poster for World War I*
4 *Winston Churchill, on the possible invasion of Britain by Germany*
5 *The Old Testament*
6 *Genghis Khan, a Mongol warrior who conquered a vast kingdom in the thirteenth century*
7 *Robert Oppenheimer, on the explosion of the first atomic bomb in New Mexico, July 1945*
8 *Ronald Reagan, who is a fundamentalist Christian*
9 *The New Testament*

– Discuss these pronouncements on war and speculate with your students on the events leading up to each pronouncement.

1 The original words were *Veni, vidi, vici*, and they probably express the ease with which Caesar conquered the Pontic States.
2 The Vietnam veteran is talking about the change that comes over a person when they are under fire.
3 The poster showed a man sitting in his living room with his two children. The aim was to shame the man into joining the army. What would his children think of him if he didn't fight to save his country?
4 This is an example of Churchill's stirring rhetoric, inspiring the people to resist any invasion.
5 This is the principle of revenge, which the Old Testament encouraged, in contrast to the New Testament. (9)
6 This illustrates Genghis Khan's blood-thirsty tyranny.
7 The scientists who had worked for a long time to produce an atomic bomb were aware that the world would be a different place after its invention and were a little fearful of their own invention.
8 Armageddon is the name given to the final battlefield between the powers of good and evil. Fundamentalist Christians interpret the Old Testament literally. The suggestion is that Reagan saw the possibility of a nuclear war between America and Russia as an opportunity for 'good' to defeat 'evil'.
9 This illustrates the passive acceptance of aggression as suggested in the New Testament.

● Vocabulary 1 (SB 53)

1 Students check the words in their dictionaries, and try to put the words into chronological order.

Answers

Ancient times *shield*
Medieval times *fortress moat helmet armour parapet drawbridge*
Early twentieth century *minefield barbed wire gas mask trench sandbag air-raid shelter*
Later twentieth century *bullet-proof vest fall-out shelter*

2 Students work in pairs to give a context to the words.

● Reading (SB 54)

Pre-reading task (SB 54)

– Students work in pairs to discuss the questions in the pre-reading task. After a while, compare ideas as a class.

Reading for information (SB 54)

– Students read the text and answer the questions.

Answers

1 *Primitive warfare is described as consisting of clashes – small outbreaks of violence between relatively few people. The battles described are between regular armies, trained, disciplined, and following the command of one leader.*
2 *It makes individuals into one fighting machine, which presumably will always obey orders unquestioningly.*
3 *Soldiers killed the enemy in front, pressed forward by other soldiers behind, and did not think at all of the people they were killing. It was their automatic instinct, executed without question.*
4 *Men in large groups will act as a mob which does not have the fears of the individuals. Almost anybody can be persuaded that they must take up arms.*

What do you think? (SB 54)

– Answer the 'What do you think?' questions as a class.

– An optional activity is to divide students into groups of three, give them a photocopy of this text and a bottle of correcting fluid, and ask them to blank out between ten and fifteen words to produce a gap-fill exercise to give to their colleagues. Encourage them to choose interesting words, perhaps collocations of adjective – noun or verb – preposition, or grammatical words such as relative pronouns. When they have finished, photocopy their blanked versions in sufficient numbers to have one between two students, and redistribute them, making sure that no pair has the gap-fill exercise that they produced. They can then check their answers with the original text.

Summary writing (SB 55)

– Students do the summary writing in class, or for homework.

▶ Language focus (SB 58 TB 37)

● Vocabulary 2 (SB 56)

| T.10 |

– This explores synonyms in English.

They (SB 56)

– Ask students to read the poem *They* quickly, and decide which war it refers to.

The answer is the First World War, although there are no particular clues in the poem why this should be so.

– Have a short discussion about the First World War to see what students know about it.

THE FIRST WORLD WAR

When was it?
1914–1918

What started it?
The immediate cause lay in a conflict of interests between Russia and Austria-Hungary in the Balkans. On 28 June 1914, Archduke Francis Ferdinand, the heir to the Austro-Hungarian throne, was assassinated in Sarajevo in Bosnia by a Serbian nationalist and on 28 July Austria-Hungary, with German support, declared war on Serbia. Russia then entered the war in support of Serbia. From there it spread through Europe and beyond.

Which countries were involved?
On one side the Allied Powers including the UK with countries of the British Empire, Russia, France, Belgium, Serbia, Italy, Japan, Portugal, the USA and Greece (both from 1917). On the other side the Central Powers including Germany, Austria-Hungary, Turkey and Bulgaria.

What characterized the war?
It was the first *world* war, whole nations not just armies were involved. There was a huge loss of life on both sides, about 9 million altogether. About 30 million men were in arms. It was the first war where more scientific ways of fighting were introduced – aeroplanes, poison gas, tanks. There was a great deal of filthy, futile trench warfare. Because of the huge loss of life and the nature of the war it was believed by many at the time that it would be the first and last world war. In fact there were just 20 years between the first and second world wars.

It has been called the last popular war – what do you understand by this?
It was the last time people generally gloried in war, either going off to it willingly themselves or sending off sons, brothers, husbands, to gain a glorious victory. It was a turning point in the attitudes of many people to war.

Gap filling   (SB 56)

– Students work in pairs to choose the best word. Encourage them to discuss the associations and connotations of the words, using dictionaries as necessary. This is not a speed activity. Encourage students to take their time.

Answers

1	*boys*	7	*boys*
2	*just*	8	*legs*
3	*cause*	9	*stone*
4	*comrades'*	10	*lungs*
5	*honourable*	11	*syphilitic*
6	*challenged*	12	*served*

Checking and discussion   (SB 57)

Questions 1 and 2
Students discuss their choices as a class, then check with the original on tape.

Questions 3 – 8
– These could be done in groups or as a class. If you think your class are forthcoming, it is often nicer to discuss such questions as a class, so everyone can hear and contribute. 'Silent' classes usually work better if one student is appointed to ask the questions and to lead the discussion while the teacher 'takes a back seat'.

Answers

3 *There are two ways of looking at war, one, that it is morally and practically justifiable, and the other, that it is a futile waste.*

4 *The Bishop thinks they will be spiritually uplifted; the soldiers say the men will be changed because of their injuries.*

5 *The Bishop sees the war as a glorious act engaged in by heroes; the fighting men know the realities and bestialities of war.*

6 *The Bishop is pompous and bombastic. His use of* **boys** *is patronizing when you read the terrible injuries they have suffered; leading attacks on Anti-Christ and challenging death sounds glorious and worthy. The soldiers express themselves in a much more down-to-earth manner. Their attitude towards the Bishop is not one of anger or complaint – they merely list what has happened to each man in a dispassionate, factual manner. The word syphilitic stands out as the one you least expect to find in a poem.*

7 *The implication is that ordinary men are fed to a war machine to keep it going. How governments get support for this is another matter, which students will perhaps have different opinions on.*

8 *He would appear to have little sympathy with the views expressed by the Bishop, if religion cannot see any of the horrors of war; insofar as the Bishop represents the Establishment, he would appear to scorn the nation that can send its men off to die; the ordinary soldier is the pawn in the game of politicians; and war is odious.*

● Listening (SB 57)

A Christmas story (SB 57)

– The listening is quite long, but it is divided up into four parts, and hopefully students will be sufficiently motivated to want to listen. In a way, it is quite remarkable that people who were present at the 1914 truce are still alive.

– Introduction: Ask students if they have ever seen the film *Oh What a Lovely War!*, or if they know what it was about.

> Sir Richard Attenborough's 1970s film is a harsh attack on war, contrasting the patriotism of those at home in Britain with the realities of trench warfare at the front. The film is in the style of a musical, with black comedy.

Part 1 (SB 57)

– Listen to the first part of the tape and answer the questions.

Answers

1 *World War I.*
2 *The British soldiers hear German soldiers singing a carol because it is Christmas Day, and they exchange Christmas greetings.*
3 *Jerry and Tommy.*

– Discuss question 4 as a class.

Part 2 (SB 57)

Answers

1 *Very similar. Graham Williams said that more carols were sung, and some together, before they started talking to each other.*
2 *The land between the two front lines.*
3 *Tommy and Fritz.*
4 *Because soldiers are trained to hate the enemy.*
5 *The two sides met in no-man's land; they exchanged presents; they helped each other bury the dead, sometimes both German and English in the same grave; they borrowed each other's tools and helped to strengthen each other's defences.*

– Discuss question 6 as a class.

Part 3 (SB 57)

Answers

1 *In some places, until New Year's Day; in others, for six weeks.*
2 *To warn the English that the friendly regiment had been replaced, so they should keep their heads down.*
3 *A friend that Harold Startin made and kept in touch with. He has been over to England to visit him.*

Part 4 (SB 57)

Answers

1 *There could be several reasons. When one thinks of the First World War, one remembers the great battles, but the Christmas Truce also deserves to be remembered; 1914 was the first year of the first total world war, and Malcolm Brown sees it as symbolic that in this year there was the greatest instance of fraternization with the enemy; also, the Truce was a protest by the ordinary soldier against the concept of war, and they were defying their governments who had told them to go and fight unquestioningly.*
2 *Never before had there been such fraternization with an enemy; we can infer that Malcolm Brown feels, given that World War I was the first global war, that this was the first instance of the ordinary citizen telling the authorities that they did not believe total war was justifiable.*

– You might want to play the tape again with students reading the script, as some of the language is quite complex, and some parts of the interview are a little mumbled.

What do you think? (SB 57)

– Answer the 'What do you think?' questions as a class.

▶ Language focus (SB 59 TB 37)

● Writing (SB 58)

– Students write about an event in the history of their country for homework. It is interesting to ask students to read their corrected essay out loud, especially if you have a multinational class. It can be fascinating to learn about the history of another country and to see its attitude to the world events. Students may need access to a reference library to check information, dates, etc.

Postscript (SB 58)

A modern war poem (SB 58)

– Students read the poem and decide who the different 'men' are.

> This is a very stark poem. The men have no feeling, no compassion, no anger or hatred. They are all like robots doing their own little part of a larger project. This might reflect the nature of killing your enemy with such a bomb, where you are thousands of miles apart and see nothing of the effects of what you have done. The message is that the machinery for dropping such a bomb is all frighteningly in place. It merely needs the word from the person responsible, that is, the leader of one of the nations who possess nuclear

weapons. *They* tells us what happens to the ordinary soldier in a close-combat war; *The Responsibility* describes how enemies no longer need face each other.

Answers
1 *Military leader*
2 *Messenger, radio operator (?)*
3 *Person in charge of air base (?)*
4 *Pilot of the plane*
5 *Mechanic*
6 *Scientist*
7 *Man in the street; you and me*
8 *Political leader*

LANGUAGE STUDY (SB 58)

T.12

1 Ways of adding emphasis (SB 58)

– Students compare the three sentences in the Language study with the corresponding sentences from the text, and read the sentences in the boxes.

Practice (SB 58)

1 Students listen to the tape, mark the stresses, and practise saying the sentences in pairs.

Answers

What annoys me most is people who are always late.

What annoys me most is the way some people are always late.

John is who you should talk to.

It is money that makes the world go round.

2 a. *What we doubt is his sincerity.*
   His sincerity is what we doubt.
   It is his sincerity that we doubt.
 b. *What I admire about the Swiss is their efficiency.*
   The efficiency of the Swiss is what I admire.
   It is the efficiency of the Swiss that I admire.
 c. *What she hates is having to get up at 6.00.*
   Getting up at 6.00 is what she hates.
   It's getting up at 6.00 that she hates.
 d. *What's important is his approval of the scheme.*
   His approval of the scheme is what's important.
   It's his approval of the scheme that's important.
 e. *What's annoying is their self-righteousness.*
   Their self-righteousness is what's annoying.
   It's their self-righteousness that's annoying.
 f. *Spain is where you should go for your holidays.*
   Where you should go for your holidays is Spain.
   (Pattern 3 sounds stilted.)
 g. *What I like about London is its beautiful parks.*
   The beautiful parks are what I like about London.
   It's the beautiful parks that I like about London.

 h. *What nobody likes is losing.*
   Losing is what nobody likes.
   It's losing that nobody likes.

3 a. *What I admire about him is the way he never makes a fuss.*
 b. *What I appreciate about her is the fact that she's always on time.*
 c. *What irritates everybody is the way this government has treated the Health Service so badly.*
 d. *What is of no consequence is the fact that the Health Service wastes less money.*

4 a. *Working until midnight occasionally is one thing, but doing it every night is (quite) another.*
 b. *Being woken by birdsong is one thing, but being woken by a pneumatic drill is (quite) another.*
 c. *Living in a caravan on holiday is one thing, but living in one permanently is (quite) another.*

5 Students work in pairs to prepare a protest talk. This should lead to some light-hearted debate as students exaggerate their case to sound emphatic.

2 Review of tenses (SB 59)

– Students work in groups of three to select the appropriate verb and put it in the right terms.

This exercise is a little more complicated than meets the eye, not in the selection of the tense but in the selection of the verb. In many cases, there is no alternative. Defences were **strengthened**; soldiers were **buried**, and they **met** in no-man's land. But there are several synonyms, or words that could well fill a gap, until you get to a later part of the exercise, when you have to go back and revise your initial decision. In fact, there are no alternative answers at all. This is explained in the answers.

Answers
a. *had been going on* (Not *to last*, because this is needed for r. *To last a lifetime* is a collocation. We don't say to *continue a lifetime or *to go on a lifetime. To continue does not fit here.)
b. *took place* (We can't say that *an event happened.)
c. *were seen* (To go on has already been used in a.)
d. *were heard* (To sing is needed in f.)
e. *joined in*
f. *were singing*
g. *met*
h. *were formed/had been formed*
i. *help* (inversion for emphasis)
j. *were buried*
k. *were borrowed*
l. *were strengthened*
m. *had felt*
n. *would/could never have happened* (To take place has already been used in b.)

o. *is now known* (There will be confusion in o., q. and u., as students decided between to *know, to think* and *to believe*. You have to arrive at the answer 'backwards'. Grammatically, all three verbs are possible in all three gaps, but not if the context is examined. In u., *to know* is impossible and *to think* is too weak, so it must be *to believe*. In q., given that the knowledge that historians had previously was inaccurate, the answer cannot be to *know*; therefore it must be *to think*. This means that the correct verb for o. must be *to know*!)

p. *continued* (*To go on* has already been used in a.; *to last* is needed for r.)

q. *thought*

r. *lasted*

s. *has been visited*

t. *have kept*

u. *believes*

v. *will be fought*

– There are three exercises on passive constructions in the Workbook.

REVISION (SB 60)

The perfect aspect (SB 60)

– Read the introduction as a class.

Practice (SB 60)

Sample answers

1 a. *We've had it decorated, and we've bought some new furniture.*

 b. *I've never tried any. Have you?*

 c. *I had spent the whole night revising for my English exam.*

 d. *she had reigned for over sixty years.*

 e. *I'll have repaired them by Wednesday night, so they'll be all ready for you.*

 f. *he had been stealing for years/he had stolen a shirt.*

 g. *What have you done to your hair?*

 h. *He had been with the same company since he left school at the age of sixteen.*

 i. *We'll have been married for twenty years.*

 j. *It has been towed away because you were parking on double yellow lines.*

 k. *It had been blown down/It had blown down in the storm the previous night.*

 l. *has been withdrawn from the market because research has shown that it can have serious side effects.*

2 a. **A** *Have you heard? The Prime Minister has resigned!*

 B *Did it say on the news why she did that?*

 b. **A** *Of course, I'm an excellent skier.*

 B *When have you ever been skiing?* (Students will want to argue that it should be *When did you go*, but **B** is expressing great surprise that **A** has at any time in his/her life been skiing, and not merely asking for the date.)

 A *Before I'd met/I met you, dear. I've done a lot of things in my life that you don't know about.*

 B *This is the first time since we've been married that you have ever mentioned going skiing. Did you enjoy it?*

 A *It was very exciting.*

 c. **A** *Who's broken/Who broke my knife?*

 B *I did. Sorry. I broke it by accident.*

 d. **A** *Darling? Have you ever met my friend Andy?*

 B *No. Hello, Andy.*

 C *Hi! I've heard a lot about you.*

 e. *I'm doing a pottery course at night school. I've learned a lot in the few weeks I've been going.*

3 When you say to hosts, as you are leaving their house, **'I've had a lovely evening,'** it is usually the use of the Present Perfect to express present interest in recent events. When Groucho Marx says **'But this wasn't it,'** he makes the Present Perfect express an event which happened some time in his life, not referring to the evening in question at all!

EXTRA IDEAS

– Literature naturally affords many texts on the subject of man's inhumanity to man. You could compare the war poetry of Rupert Brooke's *The Soldier* with any of Wilfred Owen's work. Orwell's *1984* would follow on from the work on euphemisms in Unit 4, if you showed your class part of the *Principles of Newspeak* at the back of *1984*. Joseph Heller's *Catch-22* is a very well-known book. You could show students the part in Chapter 5 where the Catch-22 is explained. Also interesting is *When the Wind Blows* by Raymond Briggs, a story told in cartoon pictures about an ordinary, old couple in the aftermath of a nuclear war.

– Speaking activities could come from your class's attitudes to nuclear weapons and protest groups such as Campaign for Nuclear Disarmament. An interesting area might be to ask students to read out loud what they write about in the writing activity in this unit (Describe an event in the history of your country).

– Listening material could come from the news, as, sadly, there is always a war somewhere. An interesting activity with the news is to use one or two stories as a dictation. Play the item once, then ask one student to do his/her dictation on the board, whilst the others write in their note-books. You can then correct the version on the board.

UNIT 6

A sense of taste

OVERVIEW OF THE UNIT

- The themes of the unit are personal taste in the decor of a room, clothes and paintings, which should provide a lot of scope for students to give their own opinions. There is a newspaper article which is a 'send-up' of how to make intelligent comments about a painting. The main reading and listening texts are extracts from George Bernard Shaw's *Pygmalion*, on which the musical *My Fair Lady* was based.

- Students are encouraged to talk about a treasured possession of theirs, and if possible, to bring it to class. This invariably leads to a most interesting discussion – hardly a 'lesson' at all – as people are naturally curious about each other!

NOTES ON THE LANGUAGE INPUT

Adjective order

Although certain rules can be given, this area is in fact quite complicated. Which adjective comes before another is sometimes to do with usage and what sounds right. Fortunately, we rarely need or want to put too many adjectives before a noun! When speaking, we often add the information in new, short sentences.

The basic rules are as follows:

Compound nouns are never separated.

coffee cup

apple tree

Adjectives that tell us what something is made of come just before these.

a clay flowerpot
a plastic garden hosepipe

Before these come words that tell us where something is from.

a Dutch oil painting
the Sydney Opera House

Before these come colour adjectives.
a black and white Siamese cat

Adjectives for age, shape and size etc. come before all these, but they do not follow in the same order by any means.

Adverbs with two forms

Students are often subconsciously aware of common adverbs with two forms, such as **most/mostly** and **right/rightly**. The others, when pointed out, cause few problems.

Adverbs and expressions of opinion

On a surface level, these adverbs seem quite straightforward, especially if they translate into the student's own language. However, their exact function can sometimes be very difficult to pinpoint, as they express the attitude of the speaker towards what he/she is saying, and one simple adverb can take a lot of explaining. For example, **anyway** means '*What I said before doesn't matter. My main point is as follows,*' or '*What I'm saying supports a previous point,*' or '*I'm going to change the conversation.*' (These are just some of the functions of **anyway**. A dictionary will list more.) **After all** means '*I am correcting you by pointing out a fact that you weren't aware of.*' If students are presented with a multiple-choice exercise where they must choose the appropriate adverb to fill a gap from a list of four adverbs, they can find their repeated errors very frustrating, and the teacher's reiterated explanation might not clarify at all. Such an exercise tests a student's ability to *recognize* the correct adverb or expression. In order to *produce* them, a much greater understanding and familiarity is required.

In this unit of the Student's Book, there is a recognition exercise and a production exercise, for which a certain understanding (albeit subconscious) is required. If you feel your students would benefit from an explanation first, do exercises 4 and 5 in Unit 6 of the Workbook before doing the material in the Student's Book.

NOTES ON THE UNIT

– Students often need to prepare what is going to be done in class prior to the lesson, but this is particularly so for some of the activities in this unit, as otherwise students will spend too much valuable class time in forming their own opinions. If you tell them in advance what you would like them to think about at home, classroom time can be spent on exchanging these opinions.

For example, before doing the first vocabulary exercise, ask students to consider the questions about their own tastes in clothes in question 3 on page 63.

A few days before you begin this unit, you could say that you will be discussing paintings, and you could ask them to think what their favourite painting is. If on the appropriate day they could bring a photograph of it to class, a most interesting discussion could ensue.

Similarly for the speaking activity on page 70, where students are asked to describe a treasured possession, it would be helpful if you gave advance warning. This is potentially a very interesting lesson, and it would be sad if it were to fail because students didn't have enough time to prepare their thoughts.

● Discussion   (SB 61)

– Introduction: Ask one or two students to describe their favourite room.

Objective descriptions   (SB 61)

– Students work in four groups to write a detailed, objective description of one of the rooms. Encourage them to use dictionaries if and when they need to. It may be necessary to keep reminding them that at this stage their descriptions must be objective. Allow sufficient time for this, about ten minutes.

– The groups take it in turns to read out their descriptions, paying attention to the introduction of any new vocabulary.

Subjective descriptions   (SB 61)

– In the same groups, students discuss their own opinions of the styles of the rooms. When you feel students have formed some opinions, open up the activity into a class discussion, finishing with a vote to see which is the most and least liked room.

● Vocabulary 1   (SB 62)

Your taste in clothes   (SB 62, 63)

– Prior to this lesson, ask your students to consider question 3 of this vocabulary exercise (on their taste in clothes) at home, so that when they come to class, they have some pre-formed opinions.

1 Discuss question 1 as a class.

2 With dictionaries, students go through the list of items of clothing, checking that they understand them and answering the three questions. There are quite a few words, so allow adequate time for this. If students seem to lose concentration after a while, ask them to check the remaining words for homework. Be prepared to do some explaining yourself, as some items will not be in the dictionary, or the definition may be inadequate.

Answer the question about items of clothing that are currently fashionable.

3 Answer the questions as a class. Depending on the interests of your class, a fruitful discussion should ensue.

● Reading   (SB 63)

Pre-reading task   (SB 63)

– Students discuss question 1 in groups.

– Question 2 will need to be answered as a class.

– Students discuss question 3 in groups.

Artspeak is an imitation of George Orwell's Newspeak, the official language of authority in his novel *1984*. Newspeak made it possible to express only what the authorities wanted people to think. The suggestion of the neologism **artspeak** is that the pronouncements about art are robotic and meaningless.

– Students answer question 4 in groups. This should raise a few laughs, and give them an idea of what the article will be about.

Reading for the main ideas

– Students read the text quickly and answer the questions.

   Answers
   1 *To train people to make intelligent comments about works of art.*
   4 *The purpose of the text is to amuse readers, and to make fun of pretentious art-lovers. To mock is perhaps a little strong.*

Text organization (SB 63)

– Students decide where the four missing sentences should go.

Answers

Sentence **a.** belongs on line 53 after ' . . . *the most tuneful pieces of 100 classical musical favourites.*'

Sentence **b.** belongs on line 4 after ' . . . *what you like or why you like it?*'

Sentence **c.** belongs on line 20 after ' . . . *works of art in public places.*'

Sentence **d.** belongs on line 63 after ' '*Insufficient,*' *says Quinn.*'

Comprehension check (SB 65)

– Students work in pairs to answer the true/false/don't know questions.

Answers

1 *True*
2 *Don't know* (He is the hero of the smart set. This doesn't mean that he is part of it.)
3 *False* (Making intelligent-sounding comments doesn't mean appreciation.)
4 *True*
5 *False* (They aren't true experts.)
6 *True*
7 *False* (They are not complete.)
8 *True*

Pairwork (SB 65)

– In pairs, students look at the pictures and decide on a title, an 'unintelligent' comment and an 'intelligent' comment. When they have compared ideas, you can tell them the real titles. They are:

> The five paintings are (top to bottom):
>
> Adolph Gottlieb (1903-74): *Blast*
> Fernand Léger (1881-1955): *The Red Statuette*
> Laurence Stephen Lowry (1887-1976): *Industrial Scene*
> Jan Steen (c 1626-79): *The Burgermeister of Delft* (right)
> Joseph Mallord William Turner (1775-1851): *Fire at Sea* (left)

▶ **Language focus** (SB 71 TB 44)

● Reading and listening (SB 66)

T.13a-c

> There are several parts to this section of the Unit, and we suggest you do the final part, **reading aloud and pronunciation**, in a different session from the rest, and with something different in between. It would be very sad if students came to do the final reading aloud exercise feeling fed up with the play, because in fact it is extremely amusing and potentially very good pronunciation practice.

– Introduction: Ask students if they have read or seen the play *Pygmalion*, or seen the musical *My Fair Lady*. Ask those who know something about either to tell the rest of the class. If no one knows anything, give them the following synopsis of the play.

> A Cockney flower-seller, Eliza Doolittle (also called Liza), is transformed into a passable imitation of a duchess by the phonetician Professor Henry Higgins, who undertakes this task to win a bet and to prove his points about English pronunciation and the class system. He teaches her to speak standard English, and successfully introduces her to social life, thus winning his bet. But she rebels against his dictatorial and thoughtless behaviour, even though he suddenly realizes he is very fond of her. The play ends with a truce between them, and she marries into society.

– Read the introduction as a class. Ask students to think of English words where the spelling is strange, where letters are not pronounced or where the same letters are pronounced in different ways. Students should have no problems thinking of examples! You could tell your class the reason for this – English spelling was fixed quite early because of printing and the first dictionaries, but the pronunciation continued to evolve. Letters that today are silent used to be pronounced.

You could also tell your class that Shaw was serious when he talked about the need to reform English spelling. He led a campaign to have English spelled phonetically, for example, **enuf** instead of **enough**.

Questions for discussion (SB 66)

– Discuss the three questions as a class. You could ask students to give some examples of different pronunciations of words in their languages.

Background to the play (SB 66)

– Read the background to the play as a class. (Higgins wants to **pass Liza off** as a duchess – this means he wants to convince everyone that she is a duchess.)

- Notice that in these extracts, Shaw doesn't always put an apostrophe to show where a letter has been dropped, for example, **thats** and **lets**. He spells 'haven't' as **havnt**. He also spells the word **show** with an **e** (**shew**), but this is an old spelling, and not peculiar to Shaw.

Extract 1   (SB 67)

- Students read Extract 1, the stage-set instructions for Act Two. Don't linger too long on the description of the room and the instruments in it. The main thing is to see what kind of person Higgins is, and then to get on to the actual play.

- Students discuss in pairs what impression they have of Higgins.

- Ask students to give you a brief description of the room.

Extract 2   (SB 67)

- Students listen and read at the same time. With this extract and the next, encourage students to enjoy the text, and not to worry if there is something they don't understand. Hopefully they will appreciate the humour of the characters and the situation.

Comprehension check   (SB 67)

- Students discuss the answers to the comprehension check questions in pairs.

   ### Answers

   1 *his ability to distinguish the difference between one hundred and thirty vowel sounds*
   2 *because he is very interested in different accents, and because he wants to help Pickering to learn how to make records of speech*
   3 *He wants to transcribe what the girl says in two kinds of phonetic script, and he wants to record her on a phonograph.*

Extract 3   (SB 68)

- Students listen to the next scene. Again, encourage them to 'sit back' and enjoy it.

- After they have listened once, they discuss in pairs the ways in which Higgins teases Liza.

   ### Answers

   He calls her names, such as **baggage**. *He calculates the amount Liza is prepared to pay him as a proportion of her income, and works out that if she were a millionaire, he would be getting sixty pounds a day. Liza can't follow this at all. He tells her not to confuse a handkerchief and her sleeve, as though she usually wipes her nose on her sleeve.*

Lingo is an informal word for **language**. **Saucy** is an informal word for **cheeky**. **Chucked** is an informal word for **threw**. When Liza says 'You had a drop in, hadnt you?' she means that he was a little drunk. 'You wouldnt have the face' means 'you wouldn't dare.' **A guinea** in old money was twenty-one shillings, which is **£1.05p**. Higgins calls her a **draggle-tailed guttersnipe**, which is a general insult meaning **a dirty street urchin**.

Comprehension check   (SB 68)

Answers

1 *Higgins is contemptuous and insulting. Pickering is kind and considerate. Mrs Pearce is very strict, and would rather not have such people in the house she looks after, but Professor Higgins, who pays her wages, insists on having such queer people in.*

2 *Because he wanted to record a new accent, but he has heard her voice before, and doesn't want any more examples of her accent.*

   His interest is revived when Pickering challenges him to have Liza 'talking like a lady' by the time of the ambassador's garden party. It is a chance to demonstrate his professional skills.

3 *She wants to pay for elocution lessons so that she can work in a flower shop, instead of working on the street.*

4 *A friend of hers has French lessons for eighteen pence an hour. She thinks that she needn't pay Higgins as much as that, because he would be teaching her her own language, so offers a shilling an hour.*

5 *He works out the amount that she is prepared to give him as a proportion of her income. If the proportion were the same for a millionaire, he would be getting sixty pounds a day.*

6 *She can't follow it at all, and complains that she hasn't got sixty pounds.*

7 *He wants her to stop crying, and offers her his handkerchief. He insults her by making out that she doesn't know what a handkerchief is for, and suggesting that she usually wipes her nose on her sleeve.*

8 *Higgins hadn't intended to give Liza his handkerchief to keep, only to borrow. In his insult, he used the words* **thats your handkerchief**. *This was meant as an explanation, but Liza interpreted it as the giving of a fine present.*

9 *If Higgins can improve Liza's accent so that he can pass her off as a duchess at an ambassador's garden party, Pickering will pay all Higgins' expenses, and also pay for Liza's lessons.*

- Students look at the tapescript and underline examples of Cockney English.

Answers

aint = haven't

She uses the verb stem instead of forming tenses sometimes. **Come** is used instead of **have come** and **came**. **Give** is used instead of **gave**.

em = them

if you was = if you were

Reading aloud and pronunciation   (SB 68)

Extract 4   (SB 68)

Characters   (SB 68)

– It is very important that students prepare this exercise for homework, otherwise too much time will be taken up in class as students familiarize themselves with the text. Set up the homework by reading the introduction as a class. Make sure students understand what is meant by 'trying her out in public'. It makes her sound like a new product or machine.

Explain that the scene is very amusing, because although she now speaks in a 'posh' accent, what she actually says is still rather common and vulgar, and she shocks the ears of her delicate audience with stories of how she thinks her aunt was 'done in', which is slang for **killed**. Students then read the text for homework, checking that they understand not only the dialogue but the instructions to the actors and actresses.

– Students read the text aloud in groups of four. Some characters have a lot to say, and some very little, so students can double up on some of the roles so that they are more involved.

Either assign or ask students to decide roles:
Student A – Liza
Student B – Mrs Eynsford-Hill /'eɪnzfəd 'hɪl/
Student C – Mrs Higgins and Clara Eynsford-Hill
Student D – Freddy Eynsford-Hill, Professor Higgins and Colonel Pickering

Students sit in groups to practise. Later, they can act it out if they wish.

There is some movement at the beginning and end, but for the most part everyone is seated.

– Go through the text as a class, sorting out any problems, and making sure that students understand certain items and can pronounce difficult words. You could draw their attention to parts of the text, and ask the following questions:

line 97   **devouring her with her eyes**
What does this mean? (Looking at her intently)
Why? (She is fascinated to meet Liza, and is dying to find out how she will perform.)

line 102   **A long and painful pause ensues**
Why? (Because they are all embarrassed, and don't know what to talk about.)
What do you think the characters do during this silence? (They probably try not to look at each other, but pretend to be interested in something else.)

line 108   **barometrical**
Check the pronunciation /bærə'metrɪkl/

line 110   **I bet I got it right**
Point out that this line is funny because it is informal, in contrast to her previous speech, which was terribly formal.

line 116   **darkly**
What does this mean? (very sinister, as though she were beginning to tell a horror story)

line 117   **clicks her tongue sympathetically**
Make sure students know what this means. It is a sort of **tut-tut** sound

line 123   **She come through diphtheria right enough**
What's wrong with Liza's grammar? (It should be **came**.)

What does come through mean? (recover from)
Point out that **right enough** is also informal, and check the pronunciation of **diphtheria** /dɪf'θɪərɪə/

line 126   **ladling**
What does this mean? (pouring from a ladle or a spoon)

line 130   **piling up the indictment**
What does this mean? (continuing to accuse people of killing her aunt)
How is Liza feeling at this point? (She's beginning to feel confident, because she thinks she's doing very well so far.)

line 130   **What call**
What does this mean? (**What reason** – this is very formal.)

line 133   **pinched**
What does this mean? (**stole**)
Is it formal or informal? (Informal)

line 134   **them as pinched it**
What's wrong with her grammar? (The people that pinched it)

line 151   **It never did him no harm**
Where's the mistake? (any harm)

line 152   **he did not keep it up regular**
Where's the mistake? (regularly)
What's funny about this line that makes Freddy snigger? (**Keep it up** suggests that

hard drinking is something virtuous and to be practised. Mrs Eynsford-Hill is appalled that Liza's father drank at all, but to Liza, hard-drinking relatives are part of her life.)

line 161   **Expansively**
What does this mean? (unreserved, willing to take)
How does Liza feel? (Very confident. She's really beginning to enjoy herself.)

line 175   **Walk! Not bloody likely. (Sensation) I am going in a taxi.**
Why is this a wonderful exit? (It's very dramatic. Liza thinks she has done extremely well, and has no idea of the shocking effect she has had on the two older ladies. Her use of the swear word **bloody**, and the pride with which she says she's getting a taxi, are a perfect illustration of the contrast in her speech – 'posh' accent with vulgar content.)

– Students practise their roles in groups. Let this go on as long as they are interested. You should suggest that roles are changed, as Liza has by far the most to say.

Pronunciation check   (SB 69)

– Students listen to the tape of the scene. Comment on the actors' performance. Ask students which actors they particularly liked, and which lines they thought were well-delivered.

– Students practise some of the parts again.

How does it end?   (SB 69)

– Read this as a class. In the film version, Liza marries Higgins.

▶ **Language focus**   (SB 72, TB 45)

● Speaking   (SB 70)

– You need to tell students in advance about this activity. If your students are living in their own country, there is more chance that they will actually be able to bring their treasured possession to class. If students are away from home, they might have to describe it instead.

– Students work in groups of three or four to describe the objects in the pictures, and to imagine why they might be important to the owner.

– Students work in groups of 4 – 6 or as a class to describe an object that is important to them. Those without objects could interview those who have treasured possessions.

● Writing   (SB 70)

– Students write one of the essays for homework.

● Vocabulary 2   (SB 71)

Adverb and verb collocations   (SB 71)

– Read the introduction as a class.

Answers

1 a. *rain heavily*
   b. *breathe deeply*
   c. *fight courageously*
   d. *explain clearly, concisely*
   e. *die peacefully*
   f. *look longingly, enviously*
   g. *argue forcefully, convincingly*
   h. *react violently, impetuously*
   i. *behave badly, correctly, erratically*
   j. *sleep deeply, soundly, fitfully*
   k. *whisper softly*
   l. *stroke gently*
   m. *investigate thoroughly*
   n. *listen attentively*
   o. *consider carefully*
   p. *progress steadily*

2 Students write some sentences to practise the above collocations.

LANGUAGE STUDY   (SB 71)

T.14/15

1 Adjective order   (SB 71)

– Students work in pairs to look at the sample sentences and try to work out some rules about the order of adjectives. Don't expect them to work everything out! As we said in the Notes on the language input, the exact rules are in fact quite complicated. They should be able to see that compound nouns are never separated, that before compounds come material and provenance, and that subjective adjectives come first. (In sentence d., **great** is an intensifying word meaning **very**, and goes with **big**. **Great** and **big** are not both referring to the size of the dog.)

– Students read the Grammar reference in class as it is not very long.

▶ **Grammar reference:**   (SB 138)

Practice (SB 71)

Answers

a. *delicious home-made brown bread*
b. *funny little old lady*
c. *blue-and-white striped silk shirt*
d. *revolting fat Havana cigar*
e. *great new metal tennis racket*
f. *plain cotton summer dress*
g. *priceless French Impressionist painting*
h. *airy, high-ceilinged living room*
i. *pretty little ten-year-old daughter*
j. *very interesting young chemistry student*

– There are two exercises on adjective order in the Workbook.

2 Adverbs with two forms

– Read the introduction as a class. There is some logic as to why one form is used and not another. The -ly adverb clearly modifies the verb. The other form, although attached to a verb, can sometimes be seen more as an adjective. For example, if you **break free**, you are as a result **free**. There is no element of **breaking in a free manner**, which is what **break freely** would mean.

Practice (SB 71)

Answers

a. *clean*	h. *free*	o. *tightly*
b. *cleanly*	i. *high*	p. *tight*
c. *clear*	j. *highly*	q. *wide*
d. *clearly*	k. *mostly*	r. *widely*
e. *easily*	l. *most*	s. *wrongly*
f. *easy*	m. *right*	t. *wrong*
g. *freely*	n. *rightly*	

– There is an exercise on adverbs with two forms in the Workbook.

3 Adverbs and expressions of opinion (SB 72)

– In this section there is one recognition exercise and one production exercise on adverbs and expressions of opinion. If you think your class would benefit from more explanation first, do exercises 4 and 5 in Unit 6 of the Workbook.

– Read the introduction as a class.

Practice (SB 72)

1 Students listen to the tape and answer the questions. This is a decontextualized listening activity, where students are denied the clues such as character, setting and background: information which normally helps us to understand a text. This means students have to listen very intensively to pick out clues that will gradually help them to understand.

Answers

1 *Four.* **You**, *who is the wife of* **him** *(who turns out to be called Jack), and the Turners. Mrs Turner is called Jane.*
2 *The husband of the woman the speaker is talking to.*
3 *She doesn't like him. She blames him for whatever it is that has gone wrong.*
4 *surveyed moving estate properties*
5 *The woman she is talking to (X) obviously lives in a house that has something major wrong with it. X's husband didn't bother to have it surveyed when they bought it. Whatever is wrong with the house has been going on for years, and it sounds as though X has walked out of the house, if only temporarily. They are still on speaking terms, by the sound of it. They might soon be looking for another house together. The speaker thinks that some friends, the Turners, should be told about whatever is wrong with X's house. It sounds as though there might be something wrong with all the houses on the estate, for example, subsidence.*

2 Students listen to the tape again and write down the adverbs and expressions of opinion, then read the tapescript and discuss their meanings.

Answers

Quite honestly *This is my honest opinion.*
Personally *This is my personal opinion.*
After all *I am giving a reason that supports what I have just said.*
I mean to say *This is what I am trying to say.*
Actually *The fact of the situation is this.*
Frankly *This is my frank opinion.*
Presumably *This is something I suppose is true.*
Seriously though *I have stopped joking, this is a serious situation.*
Admittedly *I know this contradicts what I've just said.*
After all *I am trying to persuade you by reminding you of something you know.*
Ideally *This would be the ideal situation.*
Obviously *This cannot be doubted; everyone knows.*
Surely *This must be the case, mustn't it?*
Incidentally *I am adding a piece of information that I have just thought of.*
As a matter of fact *I am adding a comment which is relevant to what I have just been saying.*
In all fairness *I think it would be only fair to do what I am about to suggest.*

3 Students work in pairs to listen to the unfinished dialogues, and complete them appropriately.

1 *Quite honestly, I don't think they're well-matched at all. She's so arty, and all he wants to do is play rugby and drink beer.*

2 *If I remember rightly, it was at Henry's cocktail party.*

3 *Presumably, they'll have a church wedding. Jane always wanted the works.*

4 *Actually, that's his brother. Paul's never been married.*

5 *After all, she's twenty-four, and she's been looking after herself quite successfully for the past six years.*

6 *Obviously, they're in love and want to start a family.*

7 *Incidentally, did you know that Henry got that new job he was going for?*

8 *As a matter of fact, they're due here in a few minutes. If you hang on, you'll see them.*

9 *Anyway, I hope they'll be very happy./Anyway, I must be going now. Bye.*

4 See 3 above.

REVISION (SB 73)

The position of adverbs

– Read the introduction as a class. You could point out that in the first example sentence, **naturally** is an adverb of opinion, or a comment adverb. In the second example sentence, **naturally** is an adverb of manner.

Practice (SB 73)

Answers

a. *I'm quite sure (I'm positive)*
   he's quite clever (He's rather clever)

b. *I never knew*
   I knew you never had

c. *Frankly, I can't answer (This is my frank opinion.)*
   I can't answer that question frankly (in an honest manner)

d. *Obviously, he realized (Of course he did)*
   He obviously realized (Of course he did)
   she obviously wasn't well (It was quite apparent.)

e. *Well, they knew (I am explaining something, or giving my opinion.)*
   They well knew (They certainly knew)
   play chess well (He was a good player.)

f *Honestly, I don't think (This is my honest opinion)*
  I honestly don't think (This is my honest opinion)
  Answer your questions honestly (in an honest manner)

g. *Only I saw him (I was the only person. This sounds rather formal. We would probably say 'I was the only one who saw him.')*
   I only saw him (I didn't speak to him.)
   I saw him only yesterday (as recently as yesterday)
   (only at the theatre is theoretically possible, but unlikely in practice)

h. *Actually, he told her (I am correcting you, or giving you a piece of information.)*
   He actually told her (I am saying that this really happened, even though it is surprising and hard to believe.)
   what he actually thought of her (He gave her his honest opinion, even though she probably didn't like it.)

i. *Still, I love you (I am emphasizing that this is the case despite what has just been said, for example, 'Peter's a nice chap.')*
   I still love you (This continues to be the case.)
   I love you still more than Peter (I love Peter, but I love you even more.)

j. *Even George (Everyone likes French cooking, even George, who is usually very fussy about his food.)*
   George even likes (This is an insult to French cooking! George will eat anything and most surprising he also likes the dreadful food they serve in France!)

k. *Very sensibly, he discussed (I think this was sensible of him.)*
   He very sensibly discussed (He discussed the design in a sensible manner, or I think this was sensible of him.)
   design with her very sensibly (in a sensible manner)

l. *I can just see (It's difficult because my vision is blocked, but I can do it.)*
   I can see just what he's doing (I can see exactly and precisely.)
   what he's just doing (What he's doing at this moment)
   (Just I can see what he's doing is possible, but sounds very formal. We would probably say 'I am the only one who can see . . . ')

– There is an exercise in the Workbook that practises the order of adverbs.

EXTRA IDEAS

- It would be interesting for the whole class to go to see an English film or play, which could then be discussed. You could teach vocabulary to do with the production of films or plays. If you are in an English-speaking environment, there will be reviews that can be read. Whether the production is seen or not, reviews can be interesting to look at in class, as they often include useful vocabulary. One task is to ask students to find the words that express positive and negative connotations, as the reviewer usually finds aspects that he/she likes and some he/she dislikes.

- The film *My Fair Lady* is available on video cassette. You could show the extracts that are included in this unit. The scene from Act Three where Liza is attempting to speak 'properly' is extremely funny. Students may want to watch the rest of the film as an extra activity.

  There is a description of a college room in chapter III of *Jacob's Room* by Virginia Woolf. You could read this (2 or 3 times) to students, perhaps omitting some of the detail about books, and ask them to visualize the room and make a rough sketch of it. Students then compare their sketches in small groups and check if they have correctly interpreted the description.

- There is a feature at the back of *The Observer Colour Supplement* 'A room of one's own' in which well-known people describe their favourite room. Unfortunately although the Observer (a British Sunday paper) is available internationally the colour supplement is not usually included. You could ask a friend in Britain to collect samples of 'A room of one's own' for you.

UNIT 7

Conscience doth make cowards of us all

OVERVIEW OF THE UNIT

– There is a theme of morality that runs throughout the unit; more specifically, attitudes to and treatment of criminals, and attitudes to violence on television. The reading text is an interview with a burglar, and there is a jigsaw listening with interviews with Kate Adie, a well-known BBC journalist, and Joanna Bogle, a member of the National Viewers' and Listeners' Association.

– There is a game, Dilemma, which tests in an entertaining (but potentially surprising!) way one's attitude to petty deceits in everyday life.

NOTES ON THE LANGUAGE INPUT

Verb patterns

Verb patterns generally were dealt with in Unit 3. This unit concentrates on verb patterns in reported speech. The introduction aims to point out that how a verb operates can be worked out from the dictionary entry, and that is often easier than looking at the code which dictionaries sometimes have. There is an exercise to practise this in the Workbook.

Conditional sentences

This unit aims to show the difference in English verb usage between fact and non-fact, and this area is dealt with further in Unit 11. First conditional sentences are based on fact, whilst second and third conditional sentences are based on non-fact. Non-fact is expressed by shifting the verb form 'backwards' in time. The Past Simple and Past Perfect in second and third conditional sentences are examples of past forms used to distance meaning from reality, and so express a hypothesis. Conditional sentences often present students with difficulties of both form and meaning.

There are many 'bits' to get right. They need to remember that **will** and **would** are rarely used in the condition clause, when their instinct (perhaps from L1 interference) is to put them in. When spoken, there are many contractions, and it is difficult for them to produce a spontaneous conditional sentence that is correct in every aspect. **Would** and **had** get confused in third conditional sentences.

On the level of meaning, the *real* condition of the first conditional and the *hypothetical* condition of the second are often confused. The third conditional is in some ways the easiest to understand, as both halves of the sentence are contrary to fact, but problems arise when students see that *mixed* conditional sentences are possible when the two clauses have a different time reference.

For the above reason, you should take care in the explanation and practice of conditional clauses so that students understand the rules clearly. There is a strong case for drilling students with pattern practice drills (substitution, transformation) to help them produce the correct form and pronunciation.

NOTES ON THE UNIT
● Reading and discussion

– Introduction: Ask students what they understand by the title of the unit, which is a quotation from Shakespeare's *Hamlet*. (It means that because we know all about ourselves, especially what we have done wrong, we also know how weak we are.) Explain that this unit is about decisions on the subject of morality.

– Talk about a crime that has been in the news recently.
   What happened?
   Who was involved?
   Was anyone hurt/killed?
   Have the police found out who did it?
   What do you think the sentence should be for such a crime?

– Students read the accounts of the seven court cases, and discuss what they think the sentence should have been. Stress that they don't need to read every word of the articles, and that the task is *not* to replace the exact words. Students are now so used to being asked to fill gaps that they do it even when this is not the task! Much useful discussion should ensue.

Discussion   (SB 75)

1 Students try to match the sentence with the crime. Opinions can range wildly over which crime is the more severe, hence which deserves the harsher punishment. This might be to do with personal or national prejudices.

Some may say that the football hooligan is a relatively minor criminal, others that the judge escaped lightly. If there is disagreement, ask them to justify their decisions.

2 Tell the students the actual sentences imposed.

Answers
Former judge   *a nine-month suspended jail sentence*
The mob leader   *ten years' imprisonment*
Drink-driver   *eighteen months' imprisonment*
Boy who killed bully   *five years' youth custody*
Drug dealer   *four years' imprisonment*
Night intruder   *a fine of £110*
Double rapist   *ten years' imprisonment*

– Discuss the questions as a class.

▶ **Language focus**   (SB 81, TB 56)

● Reading   (SB 76)

Pre-reading task   (SB 76)

– Students discuss the questions in the pre-reading task in groups of four. Ask for feedback after they have had sufficient time. Question 4 especially will require some time to do well. You could write the questions that they want answered on the board, to focus the class's attention on them (as they serve as a prediction exercise and to motivate) and to refer to after they have read the article.

Reading and matching   (SB 76)

– Students read the article and decide where the ten key sentences should go. This requires detailed reading and comprehension, and is quite a challenging exercise.

Answers
1 – h (The research evidence that shows that damage is rarely caused backs up the claim that this burglar was like many others. It is

also the first mention of the book by Maguire and Bennett, which is referred to several times.)
2 – i (It is talking about the frequency of and increase in burglary.)
3 – f (Danny goes on to say that he wouldn't earn enough if he had a proper job.)
4 – b (Danny explains how easy his first job was.)
5 – e (Danny has just said that they caught the bus for a couple of miles.)
6 – j (His first jobs were empty warehouses. He goes on to describe how he burgles houses.)
7 – d (No-one suspected their ploy.)
8 – c (The boy who told the police about him was the one he did the house with.)
9 – g (Danny is talking about his 'job' and his 'career prospects'.)
10 – a (The research shows the awful effects of burglary on the victims – does Danny think about this?)

Comprehension check and inferring   (SB 77)

– Answer question 1 as a class.

– Students could answer questions 2 and 3 in groups or as a class.

Answers
2 *He isn't prepared to adopt an honest life style because he wouldn't earn enough money.*

He despises people for being so innocent and gullible that they hide their money in such a silly place.

He despises the legal system that fined him so little when he had earned so much from the robbery.

He is an extremely selfish person. His mother is prepared to pay his fines and allow him to spend his ill-gotten gains on himself.

According to his own criteria, he is extremely successful; Danny thinks the interviewer will be assessing success according to the legality of his 'job'.

Again, this shows his contempt for people, and his disregard for normal standards of decency. He sees no wrong in taking from people who already have enough.

3 *He has done his 'apprenticeship' with several hundred burglaries; and he has been to prison several times.*

4 Ask students what they know about Robin Hood, and encourage them to ask you about him! Here is some information to help you.

Robin Hood is the hero of many English ballads, some of which date from the fourteenth century. He was a rebel who lived with his 'merry men' in Sherwood Forest, near Nottingham. He and his companions robbed and killed representatives of authority, and he was a much-loved person because it was his boast that he robbed the rich and gave to the poor. His most frequent enemy was the Sheriff of Nottingham, a local agent of central government, who was cruel and reviled by the local people.

5 Ask students to answer this question in pairs, as it requires quite careful analysis of the text.

Answers

*In line 7, he says he could **hear the burglar pottering**. One normally associates pottering with doing odd jobs around the house or garden, which is a very innocent activity. At first, the writer seems to feel a certain affinity and curiosity for burglars. He even praises his burglar for being **careful, meticulous and tidy** – all virtues, and the writer seems grateful for having had such a considerate burglar. He talks about **the skill to find something of value** in people's houses, as though he admires this.*

***Sticky little fingers** is somewhat patronizing. One usually refers to children having sticky fingers, from eating sweets. Again, one can infer that the writer thinks there is a sort of naïve innocence in being a burglar. There is also a suggestion of something sticking to a person's fingers – i.e. they acquire it illegally. His first comments about Danny seem to reveal a certain admiration – so many burglaries for such a young man. However, his admiration begins to dissipate as he allows Danny's attitude to come through. Danny blames 'his mates' for his introduction to crime; he talks about burglary as though it was an honest profession; he despises ordinary people for being so gullible; he prides himself on not making a mess.*

*It is towards the end of the article that the writer's true feelings come out. He says **'Danny leans back in his chair'**, which suggests a very confident, superior attitude. He has **all the trimmings of a pop star**, but gained illegally. (Trimmings are usually the extra bits and pieces, for example, to a certain meal, turkey with cranberry sauce, stuffing, roast potatoes, etc.) What he wants from life are material things only. He seeks no spiritual rewards. He feels that he has a right to extract from other people the means to meet his high demands, and it is probably this which appals the writer most.*

● Vocabulary 1 (SB 78)
Informal language (SB 78)

Answers

1 *mates – friends*
  quid – pound
  money for old rope – money easily obtained

blew the money – spent the money recklessly
hit the jackpot – have great success
stashed – hidden
a grand – a thousand pounds
grassed on me – informed the police
the coppers – the police
the bottle – the courage
bent – dishonest, corrupt
stacks of dough – lots of money
broke – with no money

2 *the loo – the toilet*
  uptight – nervous and jumpy
  booze – alcohol
  thick – stupid
  a rip-off – when you have been charged too much for something, or when you have been cheated generally
  hassling – annoying
  pinched – stole (n)
  What a drag! – What a nuisance/pity!
  heavy – serious and difficult to cope with
  hang-ups – inhibitions, obsessions

3 a. *bone*   e. *sick*
  b. *boiling*   f. *fast*
  c. *solid (A person can   g. *stiff*
     be frozen stiff, but   h. *stone*
     not an ice-cream.)*   i. *brand*
  d. *wide*   j. *stiff*

▶ Language focus (SB 82, TB 56)

● Listening (SB 78)

T.16a-b

– Introduction: Ask students if they watched television last night, and talk about what they like to watch.

Pre-listening task (SB 78)

– Discuss questions 1 as a class, but ask students to work in small groups to answer question 2, as it should provoke some interesting debate. After a while, ask for feedback.

– Discuss questions 3 and 4 as a class.

Jigsaw listening (SB 78)

– Divide the class into two groups. Students read the appropriate introduction and listen to their interview. When they have listened, encourage them to discuss their answers within their groups first, so that when they find a partner from the other group they are sure of their information.

– Students pair up to swap information.

Answers

1 *Joanna Bogle finds programmes which exploit sexuality offensive and harmful. She thinks that some men have revolting attitudes towards women, and this has had serious side-effects. She quotes AIDS. She dislikes such programmes because of the effect both on her (she feels offended) and on others. She doesn't say if such programmes should be banned completely. She says that her association is more concerned about violence, and she quotes the films Sebastiane and Jubilee, where people were seen being the victims of cannibals. She is worried about the effects such programmes have on other people, and she feels they shouldn't be shown on television but in private clubs.*
Kate Adie dislikes gratuitous violence and horror films, especially those where bodies are mutilated. She dislikes them because of the effect on herself – they make her feel sick. She says she wouldn't stop other people watching them.

2 *Joanna Bogle doesn't think people do know the difference between fantasy and reality, and says it doesn't always matter. She quotes The Archers, where listeners sent in clothes for a fictitious new-born baby, and Coronation Street. (They are both extremely popular, long-running soap operas. The Archers concerns country people and country life in the village of Ambridge. Coronation Street is set in a town in Lancashire, and concerns the people who live in a terraced street called Coronation Street.)*
Kate Adie feels that most people can distinguish between fantasy and reality. She doesn't say if she thinks this is important or not. She quotes three soap operas, Coronation Street, The Archers and Emmerdale Farm (which is a television soap opera about farming people).

3 *Joanna Bogle says that it does both, but concludes that it influences more than it reflects. She quotes impressive events on television which have moved or uplifted us.*
Kate Adie says that television influences behaviour and fashion, but thinks that mainly television is a reflection of our society. She thinks that it does have a positive as well as a negative influence, but that people don't imitate everything they see.

● Writing (SB 79)

– It is important that students discuss the statistics in class before writing their report, as the information in such statistics is usually very dense. The statistics should provide the basis for a good discussion. It is always interesting to compare the habits and institutions of different countries.

– Students choose a title and write their report for homework. Tell them that they should include information from the statistics only where relevant – it is not obligatory!

● Speaking (SB 80)

Dilemma! (SB 80)

– Photocopy the cards and cut them up. There are sixty in all. Students should have either 2 or 3 cards each, so that they have a choice, but make sure that there are sufficient left in the pack to distribute more as the game goes on. For classes of 20 or less play as a class. If more than 20, divide the class into 2 groups.

– Read the introduction and the instructions to the game.

> You could give an example by saying, 'Imagine I have the card about the taxi driver. I think Maria is basically a very honest person, and I think she would take the money to the police station. I don't think she would keep it. So I write down Maria would take the money to the police station. When it is my go, I read the card to Maria, and she has to tell me what she would do. If she says what I have written, I score the point. If she says something different, I can challenge her by saying how *I think* she would react.'

– Students must be sitting so they can all see each other. Ask the first student to begin. When he/she has asked another student and the discussion has finished, give him/her another card. The next student then asks a question, and so on round the room.

– The majority of the actual speaking will come when student A (the questioner) challenges what student B says he/she would do, and when student B has to defend him/herself. Naturally, the rest of the class can join in.

– In order to generate class discussion or to defuse conflict say, 'OK, let's look now not at what B **would do** but at what B or someone else **should do**.' The class can vote on the best course of action following the discussion.

> Inherent in this game is the use of the second conditional, as all the situations and reactions are hypothetical. Notice that in the situation on the cards, tenses for fact (not non-fact) are used, but then the question is always **What would you do/say?** You should insist on students using correct conditional forms. There should be lots of result clauses (suppressed conditions, because the hypothetical situation is known to all) and short answers.
> *I'd give it back.*
> *I wouldn't. I'd keep it.*
> *I don't think you would. I think you'd try to find out who it belonged to.*

SITUATION 1

You have been to a party with a friend, who is supposed to be driving you home. It is late at night and time to go home, but you think your friend has had too much to drink, even though he/she insists he/she can drive all right.

What would you do?

SITUATION 2

You are in a hotel lobby. You see someone approaching the door with heavy bags, so you open the door. The person gives you £5, obviously mistaking you for the hotel doorman.

What would you do?

SITUATION 3

You are looking for a house to buy. You find a beautiful one which is really quite cheap. Then you learn that it is supposed to be haunted.

What would you do?

SITUATION 4

Your neighbour, Henry, is having a row with his wife. Henry asks you a favour. 'If my wife asks where I was last night, say I was with you, OK?'

What would you do?

SITUATION 5

You are having a dinner party at your house. A husband and wife that you have invited suddenly begin to have a violent argument.

What would you do?

SITUATION 6

You have booked a holiday with your family on a remote, exotic island. Just before you're about to go, you hear on the news that there have been some outbreaks of violence between rival political factions on the island.

What would you do?

SITUATION 7

You are at a party. You meet a man/woman who you fall instantly in love with. At the end of the party, the man/woman proposes that you get married immediately.

What would you do?

SITUATION 8

You have invited several people to your house for a meal. One of them, you know, is a strict vegetarian. You prepare some soup, then realise you used a chicken stock cube in its preparation. It is too late to do anything about it.

What would you do?

SITUATION 9

You are in the street. You see a mother beating her four-year-old child.

What would you do?

SITUATION 10

You have been invited to a very posh dinner party. You are eating your meal when you discover a dead beetle in it.

What would you do?

SITUATION 11

You have arranged to meet a friend to go out for the evening. You wait at the pre-arranged spot. He/She finally turns up three-quarters of an hour late.

What would you say?

SITUATION 12

You are in an exotic restaurant. Not knowing what to order, you ask for the same as what someone at the next table is having. It looks delicious. When yours arrives, you ask the waiter what it is. 'Fried worms' comes the answer.

What would you do?

SITUATION 13

You are on a bus. Someone is listening to music on a personal stereo system, and without knowing it, singing out very loud.

What would you do?

SITUATION 14

At a formal social gathering, a friend introduces you to some guests. In the introduction, he/she exaggerates the facts and says many things about you which aren't true, but it sounds very impressive.

What would you say?

SITUATION 15

You have just had a meal in an expensive restaurant. The bill comes, and you realize you have no money and no credit cards on you.

What would you do?

SITUATION 16

You get on a train, anxious to find a seat as you feel weary. There is only one seat free, next to a drunk who is singing and shouting abuse at the other passengers.

What would you do?

SITUATION 17

You are at an airport. Suddenly a well-dressed stranger approaches you. He/She explains that his/her money has been stolen, and asks to borrow £20 to get home, with a promise of repayment.

What would you do?

SITUATION 18

You have been playing roulette at a casino, and have won over £1,000. If you bet it all and won, you might not have to do another day's work in your whole life.

What would you do?

SITUATION 19

You are going round a supermarket, when you see an old man, who is obviously not well-off stealing a tin of peas.

What would you do?

SITUATION 20

You have had a serious row with your boyfriend/girlfriend/husband/wife. It is his/her birthday today.

What would you do?

SITUATION 21

You are having a short taxi ride. The driver insists on telling you his political views, which are of an extreme nature and totally the opposite to your own.

What would you do?

SITUATION 22

You arrive home one afternoon, open your front door and come face-to-face with a burglar.

What would you do?

SITUATION 23

A friend of yours has a small baby. You are at her house. She is very busy, and asks you to change the baby's nappy. You have never done this before.

What would you do?

SITUATION 24

You have been standing in a queue, patiently, along with several other people, when an old lady elbows her way in front of you.

What would you do?

SITUATION 25

You have fallen out with your neighbour, and are not on speaking terms any more. One day, you are going out when you see your neighbour's front door open. You know no-one is in — he/she must have forgotten to close the door.

What would you do?

SITUATION 26

You have invited some friends to your house for a meal. You go to quite a lot of trouble to prepare something special. When the friends arrive, they ask if they could have their meal in front of the television, as their favourite programme is on.

What would you do?

SITUATION 27

Your boyfriend/girlfriend/husband/wife has just bought some new clothes, which he/she thinks are wonderful. You think they look ridiculous.

When asked for an opinion, what would you say?

SITUATION 28

You are an employer. You recently took on a new employee, who is doing very well. Then you discover that he/she has a criminal record for deceit which wasn't revealed on his/her application for the job.

What would you do?

SITUATION 29

You are driving at night. It is very cold and wet. Suddenly you see a hitchhiker, looking shabbily-dressed and tottering on his feet.

What would you do?

SITUATION 30

You are at a friend's house. His/Her six-year-old son sticks his tongue out at you.

What would you do?

SITUATION 31

Your sixteen-year-old son/daughter has expressed her/his intention to hitchhike around the world for a year.

What would you do?

SITUATION 32

You have been invited to a fancy-dress party. You arrive, looking outrageous, to find that it isn't a fancy-dress party at all. Everyone is very smart and elegant.

What would you do?

SITUATION 33

You are on a train, in a non-smoking compartment. The person opposite you has just lit up a cigarette.

What would you do?

SITUATION 34

You are in a restaurant. You have been kept waiting for some time, when the waiter appears and goes to the table of someone who arrived after you.

What would you do?

SITUATION 35

Your ten-year-old child is being bullied at school.

What would you do?

SITUATION 36

You are just settling down to a long, peaceful train ride with a good book, when a stranger comes up and says, 'Hi! I'm Pat. Mind if I join you?'

What would you do?

SITUATION 37

You have enrolled at a new language school. At the very beginning of the first lesson, your teacher comes in and says 'I want you all to take off your shoes, lie on the floor, close your eyes and relax.'

What would you do?

SITUATION 38

You enjoy painting as a hobby, but have never been very good at it. You have just finished a landscape when a stranger approaches you and says 'What a beautiful painting! How much do you want for it?'

What would you say?

SITUATION 39

You are offered a prestigious new job with an excellent salary. However, it entails spending six months a year out of the country, away from your family.

What would you do?

SITUATION 40

You open the morning post. The first letter contains an unexpected cheque for £500. The second letter is a charity appeal for a famine that is killing hundreds of people every day.

What would you do?

SITUATION 41

A colleague at work is drinking too much.

What would you do?

SITUATION 42

You go to work wearing brand-new clothes, which you are very proud of. Your boss says, 'It's about time you got some new clothes. We need to create a good impression for our customers.'

What would you say?

SITUATION 43

Someone begins telling you a joke that you've heard before.

What would you do?

SITUATION 44

An eighteen-year-old friend of yours wants some advice. 'I am passionately in love. Do you think I should get married?'

What would you say?

SITUATION 45

You are in the street. Some people in front of you are dropping all the litter from their take-away hamburger.

What would you do?

SITUATION 46

You have been round a wonderful museum. Entrance is free, but on the way out there is a sign asking for voluntary contributions.

Would you give any money?

SITUATION 47

A five-year-old child asks you, 'Does Father Christmas really exist?'

What would you say?

SITUATION 48

A five-year-old child asks you, 'Where was I ten years ago?'

What would you say?

SITUATION 49

Yesterday evening you went to your favourite restaurant. During the night you were violently ill. You are sure it was food poisoning and you think it was something you ate at the restaurant.

What would you do?

SITUATION 50

In your attempt to impress a boy/girl who you want to get to know, you have said that you are a very good tennis player, which is not true. He/She later invites you to spend the weekend with some friends. You are over the moon. Then he/she says 'Bring your tennis racket. They've got a tennis court.'

What would you do?

SITUATION 51

You have played tennis with the same friend many times, and never succeeded in beating him/her, much to your frustration. Finally, after a long game, you have match point. Your opponent hits the ball and it lands just on the line. If you call it out, you will win the match.

What would you do?

SITUATION 52

You have just come out of a supermarket. You suddenly realize that by mistake you put into your shopping bag an item to the value of £1.50 whilst going round the shop, and so you weren't charged for it.

What would you do?

SITUATION 53

When your bank statement arrives, you see that you have been credited with an extra £200 that you know is not yours.

What would you do?

SITUATION 54

There is a General Election in your country. One of the candidates is speaking on television about his/her childhood. You in fact went to the same school, and know that a lot of what he/she is saying is a lie.

What would you do?

SITUATION 55

The police are about to tow your car away because it was parked illegally. One of the policemen seems to suggest that if you offered him a bribe of £15, he would let you off.

What would you do?

SITUATION 56

You are desperate for work. You see an advertisement that asks for previous experience that you don't have, but you think you could do the job anyway. If you pretended you had previous experience, you feel pretty sure you would get the job.

What would you do?

SITUATION 57

Your boss praises you for an enterprising idea, and gives you a pay rise. In fact, the idea came from your deputy.

What would you do?

SITUATION 58

You are due to sit an important exam. You are waiting in a tutor's office when you happen to see a copy of the exam paper.

What would you do?

SITUATION 59

You see a fight in the street. There is nobody else about.

What would you do?

SITUATION 60

Your boyfriend/girlfriend/husband/wife keeps a diary that you are never allowed to see. Usually it is kept hidden, but one day you find it on the table.

What would you do?

● Vocabulary 2 (SB 80)

T.17

– This explores the relationship between spelling and pronunciation and practises word stress.

Rhyming words (SB 80)

– This activity is designed to be an entertaining exploration of words students know and words they don't. What often happens is that they begin by putting down the words they know (which is easy), but then start to make words up, thinking of a possible spelling and checking in the dictionary to see if such a word exists.

Sample Answers

a. *rake, wake, fake, lake, sake, break/brake, shake/ sheik, quake*
b. *leak/leek, peek, teak, beak, tweak, freak, reek, seek/Sikh*
c. *leer, cheer, mere, near, weir/we're, tear* (in your eye), *veer*
d. *bare/bear, care, hare/hair, lair, tear* (your clothes), *fair/fare, mare, dare, blare, rare*
e. *wane, main/mane, lain/lane, chain, cane, stain, vain/vane*

A poem (SB 80)

1 Students practise the poem in pairs first to try to work out the pronunciation of the more difficult words. Students have particular problems with the following words:

psychology /saɪˈkɒlədʒɪ/
psychiatry /saɪˈkaɪətrɪ/
psychiatrist /saɪˈkaɪətrɪst/
iron /aɪən/
advertisers /ˈædvətaɪzəz/
advertisements /ədˈvɜːtɪsməntz/
drought /draʊt/
soot /sʊt/

– Ask two or three students to take it in turns to read the poem aloud, with the other students correcting any mistakes.

2 Students listen to the poem on tape to check their pronunciation. You could ask them to practise the poem once more in pairs.

3 Students match the words to the correct stress pattern.

Answers

1 O o *ration, never, nation, complex, other, iron, lion, leisure, useful, pleasure, creature, daughter, muscle, silent, ribbon, perfect, English*

2 o O *prefer, address, possess, pronounce, towards*

3 O o o *preferable, comfortable, vegetable, architect, advertise, accident, ignorant, relative, muscular, signature*

4 o O o o *psychology, psychiatry, psychiatrist, advertisements*

5 o O o *remember, relation, creation*

6 O o o o *advertiser*

7 o o O o *accidental*

8 o o o O o *pronunciation*

LANGUAGE STUDY (SB 81)

T.18

1 Verb patterns (SB 81)

– This shows students what information about verb patterns is given in the dictionary entry.

– Read the introduction and explanation as a class.

– Read the Grammar section in class. It is not very long, and students need to have read it to answer question 2 in the Practice exercises.

▶ **Grammar reference:** (SB 139)

Practice (SB 82)

Answers

1 a. *of*   f. *on*
  b. *for*   g. *on*
  c. *for*   h. *of*
  d. *about*   i. *for*
  e. *about*   j. *on*

2 a. *She reminded Peter to pay the phone bill in case they got cut off.*
  b. *James Last denied having any involvement in the bank robbery.*
  c. *He congratulated Sheila on the birth of her son.*
  d. *She admitted to Henry that she hadn't always told him the whole truth, but she insisted that she had never told him a lie.*
  e. *John suggested that Joanna should take/encouraged Joanna to take the job in America, and offered to pay her air fare.*
  f. *Lisa complained to her husband about the weather, and blamed him for wanting to come to Scotland in winter.*
  g. *Malcolm pointed out that they had come to Scotland because she had insisted on visiting friends there.*

h. *The bank manager suggested that Alice should open a second shop, and offered to lend her the capital.*

i. *Alice reminded him that she already had debts of over ten thousand pounds, and pointed out that the market wasn't big enough for two shops.*

Listening and writing (SB 82)

– Students listen to the interview between Alison Barron and James Dunlop, and write a report of the meeting. This could be done in class or for homework. You could ask them to write the report from the viewpoint of Alice reporting back to her board or James reporting back to his union members.

Answers

Alice Barron, the Director of the company, offered to give her staff a five per cent pay rise and explained to James Dunlop, the union representative, that profits were lower than expected. James Dunlop complained that at the beginning of the year she had promised it would be at least eight per cent, pointing out that the current rate of inflation was ten per cent per year. He argued that most of the workforce could hardly afford to pay their bills.

Ms Barron accepted that the situation was difficult, and, adding that she was not prepared to increase the offer, apologized again. She explained that without capital for research and development, the company would have no future. Mr. Dunlop accused her of trying to keep the pay rise as low as possible, and warned her that there could be a strike. She suggested that he should talk to the staff and then come back, which he agreed to if she was prepared to negotiate. She accepted, and promised to see what she could do.

– There are two exercises on verb patterns in the Workbook.

2 Conditional sentences (SB 82)

– Students will have quite a familiarity with conditional sentences already, but the exercises here are challenging, so make sure they are done thoroughly, and that all rules of form and meaning are understood.

– Ask students to read the Grammar section for homework prior to the lesson on conditional sentences.

This question allows students to see how much they know about the difference in aspect between the first and second conditional, the use of **will** in the conditional clause, and mixed conditionals. You should monitor the pair work and the subsequent feedback carefully to see how much explanation is needed to be prepared to give rules and ask a lot of check questions.

Answers

a. *These are the basic forms of the first and second conditional, that is, **If + Present Simple + will** and **If + Past Simple + would**. The difference in meaning is to do with probability. The first conditional expresses a real conditional and is quite possible. The second expresses a hypothetical condition. It is possible in theory, but probably won't happen.*

b. *B's replies again illustrate that the difference between the first and second conditional is to do with how the speaker sees the event. Both replies refer to the same future event, but in the first it is seen as possible, and in the second as impossible.*

c. ***Will** can occur in the condition clause when it expresses willingness (and is unstressed) or insistence, as here (when it is stressed).*

d. *In the second sentence, **won't** again appears in the condition clause, and here it expresses refusal (which is the negative of willingness).*

e. *The first conditional sounds more familiar when it is used as a request. Because the second conditional is more distanced from reality, it sounds more polite in a request.*

f. *This pair of sentences illustrates a mixed conditional. In the first sentence there is a basic third conditional, that is **If + Past Perfect + would have**. Both clauses refer to the past. In the second sentence, **they would have offered me the job** refers to the past, but **If I spoke Spanish** refers to the present – the fact is **I don't speak Spanish.***

g. *This pair of sentences again illustrates a mixed conditional, but with the time reference the other way round. The first sentence is a basic third conditional, but in the second, **If I had accepted the job** refers to the past, and **I would be in Spain now** refers to the present – the fact is **I am not in Spain.***

h. *The first sentence illustrates how a mixed conditional can refer to the future, when the result clause with **would** expresses a future event which is contrary to fact i.e. it will not happen. **I would come with you tomorrow** refers to the future (**but I won't**); in the clause **if I hadn't already arranged to go to Paris**, 'arranged' refers to the past (**but I did arrange it**). The confusion arises because the verb action **arrange** is in the past, but the verb action **go** is in the future. The second sentence is a second conditional. As in the first, **would** expresses a future action which won't happen, and in the condition clause there is the **going to** future in its past form to express unreality (**but I am going to Paris**).*

i. *The first sentence is a mixed conditional, third and second. The second sentence is the same, but with a verb in the continuous in the result clause (**would be earning**).*

▶ **Grammar reference:** (SB 139)

– Reread the Grammar section in class if necessary, and encourage students to ask questions if they have any problems. There is a lot of information.

1 Students work in pairs to complete the conditional sentences. When you have corrected them, it might be worth drilling the sentences for fluid, accurate production with good pronunciation and correct contracted forms. You could even give some oral drills where they have to make a suitable conditional sentence spontaneously from your prompts, for example:

We brought the map. We didn't get lost.
If we hadn't brought the map, we'd have got lost.

Notice the pronunciation of the result clause.

/wiːdəv gɒ(t) lɒst/

Other examples of such prompts are:

I don't know John, so I can't introduce him to you.

I have never been to America, so I don't know what New York is like.

I haven't got any money, so I didn't buy you a birthday present.

Answers

The numbers in brackets tell you which conditional the two clauses are.

a. *If we had brought the map with us,*
 we would know (3, 2)
 we wouldn't have got lost (3, 3)
 we would have arrived by now (3, 3)
b. *I'd go to the party*
 if someone had told me (2, 3)
 if I knew who else was going (2, 2)
 if I didn't have (2, 2)
 if I weren't going (2, 2)
c. *If I knew anything about cars,*
 I could tell (2, 2)
 I would have repaired (2, 3)
 I wouldn't have bought (2, 3)
d. *If it weren't raining,*
 we could go (2, 2)/could have gone (2, 3)
 we would/could be playing (2, 2)
 we wouldn't be sitting (2, 2)

2 a. *would have enjoyed*
 b. *had*
 c. *I would have studied*
 d. *studied*
 e. *work/am working*
 f. *would have been* (if **being a doctor** is no longer a realistic ambition)
 would be (if **being a doctor** is still a realistic ambition)
 g. *were/had* (same reasons as f.)
 h. *would be earning*

i. *am* (short form of the Present Continuous **am earning**)
 do (substitute form of the Present Simple **earn**)
j. *I'm driving*
k. *Will/Would it be*
l. *would* (The second conditional sounds better, although the first is possible.)
m. *took*
n. *posted*
o. *give*
p. *tell*
q. *I'll deliver*
r. *Would you mind* (The first conditional is possible, but the second sounds more polite.)
s. *came* (second sounds more polite.)
t. *could*
u. *won't/wouldn't* (Grammatically speaking, this should be **won't** as the fact is there isn't room, but it sounds rather blunt and direct, and **wouldn't** again has a distancing effect which makes the refusal sound softer.)

– There are four exercises on conditional sentences in the Workbook.

REVISION (SB 83)

Get

Get

– Introduction: Ask students to write down four sentences using the verb **get**. In the feedback, ask if they can think of a paraphrase.

1 Students rephrase the sentences with **get**.

Answers

a. *had*
b. *have/possess*
c. *entered*
d. *catch*
e. *escape*
f. *fetch*
g. *was caught*
h. *received/was given*

2 Students write some sentences to illustrate the meaning of **get + a preposition** used literally.

Sample Answers

What are you doing in that tree? Get down immediately!
The traffic was awful. We didn't get back until midnight.
Sorry, I'm blocking the corridor. Can you get by?
The grass is wet. I'd get up if I were you.
That's my seat. Get off.

There's a pen under the settee. How did it get under there?
The thieves got in through the kitchen window.
He got on his bike and rode off.
The prisoner got over the wall and escaped.
How did the budgie get out?
We try to get away at the weekend.
I got through the dark forest as fast as I could.

– Students think of some metaphorical uses of **get + an adverb** or **preposition** where the meaning is not far removed from the literal use.

I get by on £30 a week.
We get through twenty pints of milk a week in this family.
Let's get down to business.
She tried hard to get her message across.
This weather gets me down.
The Labour Party got in with a majority of forty-two seats.
Get on with your work.
I'm trying to get through to Mr Smith. His extension is 3221.

EXTRA IDEAS

– Supplementary reading and speaking material could come from topics that are currently in the news. These might be reports of recent crimes, or controversial sentences of criminals, or the treatment of criminals, or the debate over capital punishment. More broadly, you could deal with any topic that requires an ethical decision.

– See if you can find some supplementary reading on the subject of television. This could lead to some interesting discussions on the role and place of television in our lives. It might be interesting to compare an evening's TV output in Britain with that of the students' own country, using a newspaper TV guide. *The Times* has a concise, informative guide.

– Additional listening materials could be made of English-speaking friends on either their attitudes to the issues raised in the unit (Do they agree with the sentences imposed in the seven court cases? Who do they agree with on the subject of television violence, Kate Adie or Joanna Bogle?), or other issues which require an ethical decision.

UNIT 8

Storytime

OVERVIEW OF THE UNIT

– There is a theme of story-telling that runs throughout the unit. There are two examples of Roald Dahl's work, an adaptation of the traditional fairy story *Little Red Riding Hood* and an abridged version of a short story, *Parson's Pleasure*. This might inspire your students to read more of Roald Dahl, who is a master story-teller.

– There is an interview with Barbara Cartland, a romance writer, who is in *The Guinness Book of Records* for being one of the most prolific writers of all time.

NOTES ON THE LANGUAGE INPUT

Time clauses in the past and future

This language focus concentrates on the relationship between Past Simple and Past Perfect, and Past Simple and Past Continuous. It should largely be revision for students, but they sometimes find it difficult to know when the Past Perfect is essential and when it is optional.

Time clauses in the future

This, too, is largely revision. It points out the relationship between the Present Simple and the Present Perfect in the subordinate clause; also, that, as in the first conditional sentences, **will** is rarely used in the subordinate clause.

Review of tenses

This revises tenses generally, including Present Perfect, Past Perfect, future forms, and tense usage in subordinate clauses.

NOTES ON THE UNIT

● Discussion (SB 84)

– Introduction: Ask students what sort of stories they used to read when they were young, and what their parents read to them.

1 Students look at the cartoons and discuss which famous story they are based on.

Rapunzel

A man and his wife desperately wanted children, but had none. Next door lived a witch, who grew lettuces in her garden. The wife wanted a lettuce, so the husband stole one. The witch caught him. She predicted that the couple would have a child, but she (the witch) would take it as soon as it was born. A baby girl arrived, and they called her Rapunzel. The witch took her away and kept her in a tower with no door. The girl grew up to be a beautiful lady. Every day, the witch brought her food, and in order for her to enter the tower, Rapunzel let her long hair down and the witch climbed up it. One day, a prince saw this happening, and when the witch had gone, shouted, 'Rapunzel! Rapunzel! Let down your hair!' They fell in love, and he rescued her.

The Pied Piper of Hamelin

The Pied Piper (pied means of different colours) was hired by the mayor of the town of Hamelin in Germany to rid the town of rats. He did this by bewitching them with his pipe playing. The mayor then refused to pay him, so he did the same with the children, and they all disappeared into the mountains.

Humpty Dumpty and Little Red Riding Hood

The cartoonist has put the two together, although they belong to separate stories. Humpty Dumpty comes from a nursery rhyme. He is an egg who falls

---

off a wall, and 'All the king's horses and all the king's men, Couldn't put Humpty together again.'

Little Red Riding Hood is a young girl whose grandmother is eaten by a wolf. The wolf puts on the grandmother's clothes and waits for Little Red Riding Hood. 'What big eyes you've got, Grandma,' says the girl. 'All the better to see you with,' replies the wolf. 'And what big teeth you've got.' 'All the better to eat you with!' shouts the wolf. In one version of the story Little Red Riding Hood runs out of her grandmother's house, and the wolf is killed by the girl's father. In another, she is eaten 'whole' and rescued when the wolf is killed by a hunter.

The goose that lays the golden eggs

This is from Jack and the Beanstalk. Jack sells his family cow for a magic bean, which grows and grows. Jack climbs up the beanstalk to where a giant and his wife live. The giant has a goose that lays golden eggs, which Jack steals. Eventually, he chops down the beanstalk and kills the giant.

The king who couldn't laugh

A king had lost the ability to laugh and challenged everyone in his kingdom to make him laugh. Many people tried but failed, until one person succeeded.

Robinson Crusoe

Robinson Crusoe is the character in Defoe's story of the man shipwrecked on a desert island for several years. He is befriended by Man Friday.

Snow White and the Seven Dwarfs

Snow White's mother dies, and her father remarries, but the step-mother hates Snow White. The step-mother has a mirror which she puts a question to every day. 'Mirror, mirror, On the wall, Who is the fairest of them all.' The mirror usually says that she is, but one day it says 'Snow White.' The step-mother orders that Snow White be killed, but the man ordered to do this cannot bring himself to. Instead he leaves her in the forest, where she is adopted by seven dwarves. When the step-mother again asks the same question to the mirror, it again replies 'Snow White'. The step-mother sets out to find her and poisons her with a doctored apple. Snow White loses consciousness for many years, and is finally woken up when a prince kisses her.

Questions 2 – 4
– Students do question 2 in pairs. Do questions 3 and 4 as a class. Hopefully, students will not feel inhibited about telling children's stories. Encourage the rest of the class to join in with further details. It is very interesting to hear the variations on the same story from different countries.

● Pronunciation   (SB 85)

T.19

Pre-listening task   (SB 85)

– Do the pre-listening task as a class. In question 1, check that everyone knows the traditional tale of Little Red Riding Hood.

Answers

Red Riding Hood   *innocent, helpless, weak, naïve, quick-thinking*
Wolf   *clever, sly, cruel, evil, cunning, greedy, cold-blooded*

3 *It is the triumph of good over evil. The innocent child is threatened by the wicked wolf, but survives.*

– Students read and listen at the same time. As with any joke, the impact has to be immediate, so the idea is that students understand the whole poem straight away.

– Answer the two questions.

Answers

In this version, Red Riding Hood is sly, cunning, quick-thinking and cold-blooded. It is arguable whether she is also cruel and evil – after all, the wolf was going to eat her up! The same adjectives apply to the wolf in this version too. He is hardly innocent and helpless!

The poem suggests that modern girls are resourceful, that they are ready to defend themselves and meet aggression with aggression.

Reading aloud   (SB 86)

– Students practise the poem in pairs.

● Writing   (SB 86)

– Students write a similar modern version of a folk tale or fairy story. It could be based on one of the illustrations on the two previous pages. They could prepare this in class, then write it for homework.

Answers

English fairy tales usually begin and end as follows:
'Once upon a time . . .'
'They all lived happily ever after.'

● Vocabulary 1   (SB 87)

T.20

Onomatopoeic words   (SB 87)

– Introduction: Ask students if they know the names of noises that animals make. It can be very funny to compare these words in different languages. Sometimes they are very different, and sound very funny to unfamiliar ears.

Examples

Cats miaow, purr.
Chickens cluck.
Dogs bark, growl, howl, whine.
Cocks go cock-a-doodle-doo.
Birds twitter.
Sheep bleat.
Horses neigh, whinny.
Mice squeak.

– Students use dictionaries to find out who or what makes the different noise.

Sample Answers

You bang a drum or a hammer.
A trumpet or a radio blares.
Bells chime.
You click your fingers; a camera clicks.
A fire crackles.
A door or floorboard creaks.
We talk about the crunch of footsteps on gravel or on snow.
You gasp with amazement or shock.
You groan if you are in pain.
A wolf howls.
A stone plops into a deep pond.
A lion roars.
Children shriek with excitement when they are playing.
Mice squeak.
Your shoes squelch when you walk in thick mud.
You tap your finger on a table.
Feet thump up and down stairs.

– Students listen to the sounds on tape and identify the correct word.

Answers

1 *roar*	10 *click*
2 *creak*	11 *bang*
3 *chime*	12 *groan*
4 *tap*	13 *howl*
5 *crunch*	14 *crackle*
6 *blare*	15 *shriek*
7 *gasp*	16 *squeak*
8 *squelch*	17 *thump*
9 *plop*	

– Discuss with students whether they think the words really sound like the sounds they represent. Again, it can be interesting and amusing to hear how different languages describe these sounds.

Practice   (SB 87)

1 Students work in pairs to decide which of the words fit the gaps.

Answers

a. *creaked*
b. *thumped*
c. *blaring*
d. *clicked*
e. *bang*
f. *gasped*
g. *howls/shrieks*
h. *roared/howled*
i. *groan/creak*
j. *squelched*
k. *clicked/tapped*
l. *chimed*

2 Students work in small groups to write a similar story.

● Reading   (SB 87)

Background information

Thomas Chippendale was a cabinet maker, born in 1750, famous for the quality and style of his workmanship. The farmers, Bert and Claud, have country accents, and their grammar is sometimes non-standard. They say **them drawers** instead of **those drawers**, **till he do** instead of **till he does**. They swear a lot – **bloody old, damn well, piddling little**. The bill is written in old English. **Thos** is an abbreviation of **Thomas. Carvd, shapd** and **chasd** are spelt **-ed** in modern English.

The commode in this story is a chest of drawers.

Pre-reading task   (SB 87)

– Read the introduction as a class. Ask students what they think a **sting-in-the-tail** means. If necessary, tell them that a scorpion has a sting in its tail. It means that a story has an unexpected, bitter or nasty ending which the rest of the story has not led you to predict.

– Students look at the ten sentences from *Parson's Pleasure*. (A parson is like a vicar without special rank.) Allow a reasonable time for them to decide what they learn about the characters, the setting and the plot – between 5 and 10 minutes.

– Ask for feedback from the groups.

Sample answers

Characters

Cyril Boggis, a dealer in antique furniture, has a somewhat dishonest way of obtaining pieces. He disguises himself as a clergyman. He seems to enjoy getting furniture as cheaply as possible and cheating people out of their possessions.

Rummins is a farm owner who owns a commode (a chest of drawers).

Setting

In the countryside in England, presumably, on Rummins's farm.

Plot

how Boggis operates his scheme, and how he gets on when he sees a valuable commode. He tries to persuade Rummins that he only wants the legs.

– Students read the story. They will inevitably finish at different times, so you can ask those that finish first either to check the words they didn't know in their dictionaries, or to begin the Comprehension check questions.

Comprehension check (SB 90)

Answers

1 *True. He happened to be inside a farmhouse after his car had overheated and he spotted two beautiful old armchairs. He then thought that he might find more valuable furniture in other farmhouses.*
2 *False. Boggis persuaded her to sell them even though she had had no intention of doing so.*
3 *False. He parked some way from the houses because he didn't want people to see that he had a large car.*
4 *True. The story doesn't say why, but presumably the wealthy know what their furniture is worth, and so wouldn't be duped.*
5 *False. He pretends that he has heart problems to cover up his amazement at seeing the commode.*
6 *False. He says he wants the legs to put on a table.*
7 *False. He tries again and again to point out that it must be old.*
8 *True. The men then wouldn't have broken it up into pieces. It could also be argued that Boggis's mistake was to be dishonest and to try to trick people.*

What do you think? (SB 90)

– Answer question 1 as a class. The moral, presumably, is that greed and dishonesty will be punished.

– Students do question 2 in pairs.

– Answer questions 3 and 4 as a class.

– An interesting way to exploit this passage is to ask students to read aloud those parts that contain a lot of dialogue. Assign the roles, and monitor pronunciation very carefully.

– There is also some interesting vocabulary, which you could write on the board with line numbers and ask students to try to guess the meaning.

Examples

line 37	carved	line 146	coveted
line 58	dilapidated	line 166	saunter
line 68	engraved	line 167	frowning
line 75	lucrative	line 200	brittle
line 86	rambling	line 219	tossed . . .
line 89	pot-bellied		contemptuously
line 93	stumpy	line 284	junk
line 93	shifty eyes	line 306	severed
line 142	layman	line 335	brow

▶ **Language focus** (SB 93 TB 64)

● Listening (SB 90)

T.21

Pre-listening task (SB 90)

– Students work in pairs or small groups to answer question 1 and try to imagine what a typical story by Barbara Cartland might be like.

– You might choose to do the gap fill exercise on page 55 of the Workbook, which is an extract from the beginning of one of Barbara Cartland's books, *The Goddess of Love*. This would give students an idea of the style and content of her books.

– Students work in pairs or small groups to think of questions they would like to ask her.

Listening for information (SB 91)

– Students work in pairs to answer the questions. Play the tape again if necessary. Students could read the tapescript at the same time if they wanted, as some parts of the interview are difficult to follow.

In the interview Barbara Cartland says that her books have been **plagiarized**, but in fact she means **pirated**, that is, unauthorized versions have been printed. She pronounces the word **era** as though it were **area**; and she says people are **fed to the teeth** when she means **fed up to the back teeth**, which is an idiom meaning **very fed up**.

Answers

1 *1923 – Her first novel was published.*
450 – She has written over 450 novels.
45 million – the number of books she has sold (a mistake, in fact she has sold 450 million).
23 – the average number of books she has written each year over the past eleven years.
18th – She is due to start her eighteenth book this year.
5 – the number of secretaries she has.
6,000 – 7,000 – the number of words she writes per day.

8,000 – the number of words she had written the day before.
2 – She tells God to give her only one plot, not two.
20 – 30 – the number of history books she reads as research for every novel she writes.

2 Because her books are illegally translated and published in other countries, which she can do nothing about.

3 Her assumption is that in the eyes of the majority of people, she, Barbara Cartland has 'got it right', and that her attitude to love and romance is shared by most of the rest of the world.

4 To get details correct, as she is used so much in schools and universities.
Logic dictates that she reads 23 × 20/30 history books per year, which is between 460 and 690. This seems a bit of an exaggeration.

5 Because when they read her books, not only do they get a romance but also a history lesson and a geography lesson.

What do you think?   (SB 91)

– Discuss these questions as a class. There are no set answers for these questions.

   Sample answers

   3 *Students could argue a case for or against most of these adjectives. She is certainly energetic, romantic and enthusiastic. She may appear to be snobbish and aristocratic. Her heroines might be prudish, but the writer doesn't come across as a prude herself.*

▶ **Language focus**   (SB 93 TB 65)

● **Vocabulary 2**   (SB 92)

Homonyms   (SB 92)

– Read the introduction as a class.

Practice   (SB 92)

– Students work in pairs to find the homonym and complete the chart. As there are so many homonyms in English, it is perfectly possible that there is more than one homonym in each sentence. This is pointed out in the answers.

   Sample answers

   b. *dock – the place in a court where the accused sits or stands.*
   We went down to the docks and looked at the ocean-going liners.

   c. *hampered – restricted, hindered*
   We packed a large wicker hamper and went for a picnic.

d. *shed – lose*
   Garden tools are stored in a shed.
   (Leaves is also a homonym.)

e. *utter – say, speak*
   The room was utter chaos with clothes everywhere.

f. *sole – only*
   Could you sole and heel my shoes, please?
   The restaurant serves excellent Dover sole.

g. *pawns – objects made use of by others for their own advantage*
   Pawning possessions used to be a common way of obtaining money in emergencies in Britain.

h. *perk (up) – become more cheerful*
   There are some good perks with this job – company car and free travel.

i. *fast – indicating later than the actual time*
   During my fast I lost a kilo.

j. *grazes – superficial injuries to the skin*
   A herd of cows were grazing in the pasture.

LANGUAGE STUDY   (SB 93)

1 Time clauses in the past and future (SB 93)

– Read the introduction as a class. Students work in pairs to discuss the five sentences with **when**.

   Answers

   1 *We'll decide on a price during the meeting.*

   2 *We'll decide on a price after the meeting.*

   3 *We decided on a price during the meeting.*

   4 *We decided on a price before the meeting.*

   5 *We decided on a price after the meeting.*

▶ **Grammar reference:**   (SB 140)

– Students read the Grammar section for homework or in class. It is not very long.

Practice

Answers

a. *Before I visit other farms, I'll disguise myself as a clergyman.*
   After I've disguised myself as a clergyman, I'll visit other farms.

b. *As soon as he returned to London, he worked out a plan.*
   While he was returning to London, he worked out a plan.
   By the time he had returned/he returned to London, he had worked out a plan.

c. *When he saw the priceless piece of furniture, he gasped in amazement.*
Immediately he saw the priceless piece of furniture, he gasped in amazement.

d. *I'll search every antique shop until I find/have found the one I want.*
Once I've searched every antique shop, I'll find the one I want.

e. *As soon as I've saved the money, I'll buy the picture.*
Before I buy the picture, I'll save the money.

f. *While he went/was going to collect his van, they chopped the drawers into firewood.*
Once he had gone to collect his van, they chopped the drawers into firewood.

g. *As they were finishing the job, he arrived to load the van.*
Before they finished/had finished the job, he arrived to load the van.

h. *Once we get/have got the money, we'll buy a new tractor.*
We won't buy a new tractor until we get/have got the money.

2 Review of tenses

Answers

1 a. *have lived* (The continuous is also possible, but has the idea of temporariness, and five years is quite a long time.)
   b. *moved*
   c. *was/had been born*
   d. *had lived*
   e. *decided*
   f. *could*
   g. *would move*
   h. *did*
   i. *have never regretted*
   j. *are reminded*
   k. *draw*
   l. *have had*
   m. *rush*
   n. *do*
   o. *are playing*

2 a. *are thinking*
   b. *has accepted*
   c. *starts/is going to start*
   d. *does/has* (**Does** is a substitute for the Present Simple; **has** is a short form of the Present Perfect.)
   e. *will have*
   f. *don't think*
   g. *realizes/has realized*
   h. *will be*
   i. *am going/go*
   j. *am*
   k. *is coming*
   l. *does*
   m. *am*

n. *have decided*
o. *am going to get*
p. *won't feel*
q. *have found*
r. *will say*
s. *hear*
t. *are moving/are going to move*
u. *have lived*
v. *would hate/will hate* (This is the difference between fact and non-fact. If it is seen as certain that they will move to a town, **will** is correct. If it is still a hypothesis **would** is correct.)

– There are two exercises on tenses in the Workbook.

REVISION   (SB 93)

Punctuation   (SB 93)

1 **Answers**
   a. The comma after **Russian** is optional.
   b. No comma after **me**. Commas are not used after verbs of saying or thinking. No question mark in reported speech.
   c. No comma after **said** for the same reason as in b.
   d. *'That,' said John, 'is all I know.'*
   'Why?' asked Angela.
   e. Correct. When the subordinate clause comes first in a sentence, a comma is used.
   f. Correct. When the main clause comes first, no comma is used. (Think of a comma as a pause when speaking.)
   g. Without commas; **who works in New York** is a defining relative clause – *I have more than one daughter.* With commas, it is a non-defining relative clause – *I have only one daughter.*
   h. *My wife, who's in publishing, is going to a book fair.*
   This must be a non-defining relative clause as I can only have one wife.
   i. *In '78 I went to America.*
   An apostrophe is used to show where numbers have been missed out.
   In the plural of numbers they are optional:
   the 1970s
   j. *Peter's.* Apostrophe with full noun for possession.
   It's yours.
   No apostrophe as this is the possessive pronoun.
   k. *a fortnight's holiday*
   Fortnight is singular.
   a few weeks' time
   Weeks is plural.
   l. *the girls' school . . . the boys'*
   Both nouns are plural.

m. With the comma, normally means **generally** or
usually.
Without a comma, normally is an adverb of
manner, telling us how she talks – she talks in an
abnormal way.

2 Students work in pairs to comment on the use of the
various punctuation marks. The uses are all
explained in the Grammar section.

▶ **Grammar reference:** (SB 141)

3 **Answers**

a. *He once received a letter from his bank manager,
who had written to remind him of an overdraft.
The letter ended with the standard phrase, 'If I can
be of any service to you, do not hesitate to call on
me.'*
*Marx immediately put pen to paper. 'Dear Sir,' he
wrote, 'The best thing you can do to be of service
to me is to steal some money from the account of
one of your richer clients and credit it to mine.'*

b. *Getty once received a request from a magazine for
a short article explaining his success. A two-
hundred-pound cheque was enclosed. The multi-
millionaire obligingly wrote, 'Get up early. Work
late. Strike oil.'*

c. *A certain Mrs Smythe, who was notorious for
courting celebrities, sent Shaw an invitation
reading, 'Lady Smythe will be at home on Tuesday
between four and six o'clock.' Shaw returned the
card with the following annotation, 'Mr Bernard
Shaw likewise.'*

d. *A lady MP once rebuked Churchill for being
intoxicated at a dinner party. 'Sir,' she said, 'you
are drunk!'*
*'And you, madam, are ugly,' Churchill retorted,
'but I shall be sober tomorrow!'*

e. *In conversation with Churchill, Lady Astor
expounded on the subject of women's rights.
Churchill opposed her on this and other causes that
she held dear. In some exasperation, Lady Astor
said, 'Winston, if I were married to you, I'd put
poison in your coffee!'*
*Churchill responded, 'And if you were my wife,
I'd drink it!'*

EXTRA IDEAS

For extra listening material, it would be interesting to
record some English-speaking children retelling their
favourite story, perhaps a fairy story, or perhaps
something modern. It can be difficult for students to
understand children sometimes, as they have not been
exposed to the way children talk. Alternatively, you
could ask some English-speaking friends to tell their
favourite joke, and then encourage your students to tell
some jokes in English. However, telling jokes in a
foreign language is notoriously difficult, and jokes do
not often cross cultures, but it is interesting to see what
another culture laughs about.

For extra reading material, you could select some short
stories for your students to read at home and then
discuss in class. Roald Dahl has written several
collections of short stories, including *Kiss Kiss* and
Someone Like You.

UNIT 9

A sense of place

OVERVIEW OF THE UNIT

- There is a theme of people's background that runs throughout the unit. There are extracts from three autobiographies, and students are encouraged to talk about their roots and what home means to them. Listening to a variety of regional accents in English leads on to discussion about national stereotypes and prejudices.

- On a related theme, there are vocabulary exercises on American English and specialist registers.

NOTES ON THE LANGUAGE INPUT

Relative clauses

The area of relative clauses is one where students' actual performance usually outstrips their conscious awareness of the rules. It is a tricky area, with large conceptual difficulties and smaller problems of form to grapple with. The hardest distinction to appreciate is between defining and non-defining relative clauses, which your students might not have heard about before. (This is an area where native speakers sometimes make mistakes, especially over whether a comma is needed when writing.) Generally, it is quite clear whether a clause is defining or non-defining.

*Where's the money **I lent you?*** (defining)
*He lent me a thousand pounds, **which was** exactly **the amount I needed** to pay my debts.* (non-defining)

A non-defining relative clause is always like an afterthought – 'Here's something else that you might like to know' – whilst a defining relative clause is a vital part of the sentence, because without it, we don't know which one. This is what a defining relative clause always does – it tells us **which one**. Defining relative clauses are much more common, especially in the spoken language, but a good grasp of non-defining relative clauses is essential in the production of full, balanced sentences when writing.

You might choose to begin work on this area with the first exercise in Unit 9 of the Workbook, which aims to highlight the essential difference in meaning between the two kinds of relative clause. After nouns such as *the Pope* or *the Tower of London*, we can expect a non-defining relative clause because we already know which one. After nouns such as *the boy* or *a place*, we expect a defining relative clause to tell us exactly which one. Sometimes both are possible with a change in meaning.

*Politicians **who deceive the public** are a dishonourable bunch of people.*
*Politicians, **who deceive the public**, are a dishonourable bunch of people.*

The first sentence gives credit to some politicians – there are some that don't deceive the public. The second damns all politicians as liars!

Having seen the above distinction, it is quite straightforward to select the right pronoun. Encourage students to form contact clauses wherever possible by dropping the pronoun, and when there is a preposition, to put it at the end of the clause.

There are four exercises in both the Student's Book and the Workbook on relative clauses. Fortunately, as was said at the beginning of these notes, students can often <u>feel</u> what is the right form! Asking them to use their ear to decide what sounds right is not a bad idea when doing these exercises.

Participles
Participles can be used as both adjectives and adverbs, but this difference is of little importance to students. They are practised in the following ways in the Student's Book and the Workbook.

- as adjectives:
  *the **setting** sun*
  *the **finished** product*

- as reduced relative clauses (adjective clauses):
  *a man **sitting cross-legged** on the floor*
  *the money **stolen in the robbery***

– in adverb clauses:

Kissing her husband goodbye, *she went off to catch the train.*
Found hiding in a garden shed, *the escaped prisoner offered no resistance.*

– after certain verbs:

I spend Sunday **reading** *in bed.*

Students will probably produce the first and fourth of these uses with no problem, but it is worth focusing on the second and third, as they are stylistically quite sophisticated.

Nouns in groups

Three common patterns of nouns in groups are practised:

– the genitive with **'s** or **s'**
the boy's bike
the boys' school

– the **of** structure
days of wine and roses

– noun as adjective (two or more nouns together)
fish shop
car repair manual

Sometimes two of the structures are possible (**the earth's gravity; the gravity of the earth**) and sometimes not (**Peter's job;** **the job of Peter*). Sometimes there is a change in the meaning (**a wine bottle** is empty; **a bottle of wine** is full; **dog biscuits** are general; **the dog's biscuits** refer to a specific dog). Usage often dictates that one form is preferable to the others, but the rules are immensely complicated! See Swan (*Practical English Usage*, OUP) 421-5 for details.

Here are some brief notes to help you.

The **'s** genitive is used when referring to a person or an animal.

John's aunt
the cat's paws
the government's policy

The first noun is like the subject of a sentence. John **has** an aunt; the government **produced** a policy.

When two nouns come together, the second word is more like a subject.

a wrist-watch (a watch you wear on your wrist)
a bus ticket (a ticket you need to travel on a bus)
a fruit shop (a shop that sells fruit)

We put two nouns together to describe a common, accepted thing that needs a special name. We talk about a **tennis ball**, a **football**, a **golf ball**, a **beach ball**, but not a * **water ball** or a * **dog ball**, because the concept isn't common enough (it might be one day). Instead, we would talk about a **ball for playing in the water with**, or a **ball that dogs play with**.

The **'s** genitive is used to talk about products from living animals when they can still in some way be attributed to the animal.

a bird's egg
cow's milk
lamb's wool

However, if the animal has been killed, or if the object no longer 'belongs' to the animal, the noun as adjective structure is more common.

Have you ever tried duck eggs?
a lamb chop
chicken liver paté

NOTES ON THE UNIT

● Pronunciation   (SB 95)

Limericks   (SB 95)

1 Read the introduction about limericks as a class.

– Read aloud the limerick about the gentleman dining at Crewe (a town in England), and ask one or two students to read it out loud too.

> Make sure students keep to the rhythm, even when this goes against normal word stress. For example, an adjective and a noun together usually have equal stress (a 'brown 'dog), but the rhythm of a limerick will override this (a large 'mouse). You could put the rhythm on the board.
>
> o O o O o O
> o O o O o O
> o O o O
> o O o O
> o O o O o O

– Ask students to practise the limerick in pairs.

– Students work in pairs to sort out the six jumbled limericks. They usually enjoy doing this, as they also have the satisfaction of laughing at the jokes.

Answers

There was an old woman from Kent,
Whose nose was remarkably bent.
One day, they suppose,
She followed her nose,
And nobody knows where she went.

There was an old man from Crewe
Who dreamed (/dremt/) he was eating his shoe.
He woke up in the night
With a terrible fright
And found it was perfectly true.

68

There was a young cannibal called Ned,
Who used to eat onions in bed.
His mother said 'Sonny,
It's not very funny.
Why don't you eat people instead?'

There was a young lady from Gloucester
(/'glɒstə/),
Whose parents thought they had lost her.
From the fridge came a sound,
And at last she was found.
The trouble was how to defrost her.

There was a young lady called Perkins,
Who was awfully fond of small gherkins.
One day for her tea
She devoured forty-three,
And pickled her internal workings.

There was a young man called Paul,
Who grew so exceedingly tall,
When he got into bed
He could stretch out his leg
And turn off the light in the hall.

When students have sorted them out, ask different students to read them aloud, paying particular attention to longer lines where all the words have to be fitted in to the rhythm! Students can then practise them in pairs.

2 You might choose to ask students to do this as homework and learn it by heart to recite to others in the class. Students can also write limericks in pairs or groups about other students or you, the teacher!

● Reading (SB 96)

Pre-reading task (SB 96)

- Introduction: Ask students if they like reading biographies and autobiographies and whose they have read.

- Students divide into three groups. Allocate one of the men (Charlie Chaplin, Muhammad Ali and Laurie Lee) to each group, choosing, if possible, according to the interests of the students.

- Students write questions about their person to ask their colleagues. Make sure the questions are well formed.

- They put their questions to the other students. If they don't know, they can ask you. Here are some notes to help you. If no-one knows the answer, it doesn't really matter, as the aim of the activity is to arouse interest. Students usually know most about Charlie Chaplin and least about Laurie Lee.

Charlie Chaplin (1889 – 1977)

A famous comedian in silent movies. He was born into a poor London family. He toured English music halls before moving to the United States in 1910, where he lived for 40 years. His most famous role was the tramp, dressed in a hat and a suit that was too large, and carrying a walking stick. Some of his greatest films are *The Kid*, *The Gold Rush*, *Modern Times* and *The Great Dictator*.

In the 1940s and 50s, he was accused of supporting communism. Chaplin went to live in Switzerland, where he lived for the rest of his life. In 1972 he received an honorary Oscar, and in 1975 he was knighted.

Laurie Lee (1914 –)

He was born in Gloucestershire (in the west of England). His poetry shows a rich, sensuous appreciation of the natural world, as does his best-known work, *Cider with Rosie* (1959), a highly evocative and nostalgic account of his country boyhood in a secluded Cotswold valley. It describes a vanished rural world of home-made wine, village school and church outings. The Rosie of the title is a village girl who 'baptizes (him) with her cidrous kisses'.

A second autobiographical volume, *As I walked out one midsummer morning*, describes his walk to London and his months in Spain shortly before the start of the Spanish Civil War.

Muhammad Ali (1942 –)

He was born Cassius Clay in Louisville, Kentucky. In 1964 he adopted the Black Muslim religion and changed his name. He was the first heavyweight boxing champion to win the title four times, which he did in 1964, 1967, 1974 and 1978. In 1967, he was convicted on charges of refusing induction into the US Army.

He was one of the most colourful and controversial champions in boxing history. He boasted about his ability and made up poems that scorned his opponents. Early in his career, he even predicted the round in which he would defeat his opponent.

Jigsaw reading (SB 96)

- Students scan the three extracts to decide which was written by who.

  Answers

  London was sedate . . . Charlie Chaplin
  The last days of my childhood . . . Laurie Lee
  I remember the summer of 1956 . . . Muhammad Ali

- Students read the extract written by the man they wrote questions about, and answer the questions. Encourage them to discuss the answers to the questions in groups so that they are sure of the answers before they re-group to disseminate their information.

Questions   (SB 96)

Answers

1 **Charlie Chaplin** *He was born in 1889, and he is describing the London of his childhood, so it must be around 1900, the turn of the century. We don't know how old he was exactly – between 5 and 12, perhaps.*

   Laurie Lee *The late 1920s, when he was 12.*

   Muhammad Ali *In 1956. He was born in 1942, so he was 14, but he is describing his childhood generally.*

2 **Charlie Chaplin** *Yes. He got a lot of pleasure from trivial things.*
   You get the impression that he was very fond of and close to his mother, and they did a lot of things together. He says that his mother had prosperous days, so presumably she had impoverished days, too.

   Laurie Lee *We presume it was a happy childhood, but we can't be sure because that is not the focus of what he is talking about. He would appear to have led a country life, with the simplicities and chores inherent in that life. As to whether his family was well-off, he describes a life of hard work with backs bent to the ground, which suggests farm work, but he need not necessarily be describing his own family.*

   Muhammad Ali *He talks about his family with tenderness, so we can infer that it was a happy childhood, but a very poor one.*

3 **Charlie Chaplin** *In London.*

   Laurie Lee *In the country.*

   Muhammad Ali *In town.*

4 **Charlie Chaplin** *His mother, who he seems to have been close to.*

   Laurie Lee *He mentions his family in the same context as his whole generation to point out the kind of world they all lived in. We don't know his attitude towards them.*

   Muhammad Ali *He mentions his brother, Rudy, his father, and Bird, who is presumably his mother. He seems to have been close to his family.*

5 **Charlie Chaplin** *Horse-drawn tram-cars; a horse-bus; penny steamers. He is describing his childhood memories of London. He says the tram-cars went at a sedate pace, just as the rest of London was sedate at that time.*

   Laurie Lee *He describes the revolution that cars brought to his world, so he mentions the horse, which for thousands of years had been the only means of transport on land. Cars, buses and motor-bikes shattered the peace of the countryside and terrified animals and old people, who had never seen such speeds. He also says that before the arrival of the car, people rarely travelled for pleasure. Distances were so great that they only travelled if they had to for work.*

   Muhammad Ali *He mentions the bus to school, which his parents could only occasionally afford the fare for. His parents could only afford an old car, and never new tyres (**tires** is American English). Both points are to illustrate how poor his parents were.*

6 **Charlie Chaplin** *He describes his childhood very nostalgically. It was a time of innocent pleasures, and he obviously loved his mother, but there is no suggestion that he was unhappier later in life.*

   Laurie Lee *Perhaps he found the arrival of the car quite exciting when he was twelve. When he writes, he seems to think that a life where the horse was king, and where roads were innocent of oil or petrol, represented some sort of natural order into which the car was an unnatural intruder. There was a silence that he perhaps now misses. However, he also talks about the world before the car as his prison which was impossible to break out of, so perhaps he also appreciated the liberating effect of the car, allowing people to travel for pleasure.*

   Muhammad Ali *He describes at length the poverty of his family, with little food and a dilapidated house, so presumably there is little that he would like to recreate.*

7 **Sample answers**

   Charlie Chaplin *Sedate London, and innocent childhood memories.*

   Laurie Lee *How the arrival of the car brought the end of a thousand years' life.*

   Muhammad Ali *The poverty of his childhood.*

– Students find a member from the other two groups to compare answers. This discussion should last ten minutes.

– Students read the other two extracts.

Questions for discussion   (SB 97)

– Questions 1 and 2 could be done as a class, as the answers are quite straightforward, whilst questions 3–5 need more time, so students could do them in pairs or small groups.

Answers

1 *Muhammad Ali's is most factual.*
   Charlie Chaplin's is most nostalgic.
   Laurie Lee's is most poetic.
   Laurie Lee's is about change.
   Charlie Chaplin's is about memories.
   Muhammad Ali's is about poverty.

2 *He is a sign painter.*
Bird, we presume, is a nickname for his mother.
Laurie Lee's parents perhaps worked the land. (In fact, his parents were separated.)
Charlie Chaplin's mother had mixed fortunes. In fact she was an actress who did not always have work. (His father was also an actor, but his parents were separated.)

3 **. . . the end of a thousand years' life.**
As he says later in line 44, the horse had been the only form of transport for hundreds (and possibly thousands) of years. This was to end when the motor-car came. The village would never be the same again.

. . . hands massaging the crops . . .
The looking after of crops had to be done by hand, such as weeding and thinning out, and this had to be done with great care to avoid damaging the crop.

. . . waiting on weather and growth . . .
They were dependent on nature, and had to learn to be patient.

. . . and almost never for pleasure . . .
The luxury of travel for pleasure only arrived with the motor-car. Before that, distances were too great, and travelling was only done out of necessity.

. . . and more people came and went . . .
This could either refer to the people of the village travelling more in the bus, or outside people coming into the village.

4 *He seems to have approved more of life before the arrival of the car. It was **a world of silence;** roads were **innocent of oil or petrol;** days had a natural **rhythm.** He also describes this life as a **prison,** so there must have been something in him wanting to escape.*

*When the car came, horses screamed, animals **were early sacrifices,** and **old folk had strokes and seizures.** In addition, this transport was unreliable, and Laurie Lee pokes fun at the boys who shot up a hill in two minutes, but **then spent weeks** repairing their motor-bikes.*

5 Students could be given a few minutes to formulate ideas followed by class discussion and leading on to their own experiences, which would form the basis of the written work below.

Vocabulary (SB 98)

Answers

a. *sedate*
b. *gay (**Gay** has largely lost this meaning now. **Gay** more often means homosexual.)*
c. *trivial*
d. *manipulating*
e. *quivering*
f. *escorting*
g. *glided*
h. *massaging*
i. *rutted*
j. *abetted*
k. *fodder*
l. *clamorous*
m. *demented*

▶ **Language focus** (SB 102, TB 74)

● **Writing** (SB 98)

Encourage students to be quite nostalgic with this activity. It can produce some very moving accounts, which, if individuals have no objection, can be read aloud to the rest of the class.

● **Vocabulary 1** (SB 98)

1 Varieties of English (SB 98)

– Read the introduction as a class.

1 **Answers**

Vocabulary
School was out   *We were on school holiday*
blocks   *streets*

Spelling
tires   *tyres*
neighbors   *neighbours*

Grammar
we had gotten   *we had had*

2 **Answers**
a. *He isn't going to help.*
b. *I've got to go.*
c. *From Monday to Friday.*
d. *Did you have a good holiday?*
e. *Boy, he was really angry!*
f. *Do you want a biscuit?*
g. *I arrived in the autumn.*
h. *Waiter! The bill, please.*
i. *I'm going to the town centre.*
j. *What did you do at the weekend?*

2 Specialist registers (SB 98)

– Read the introduction as a class.

– Students use their dictionaries to look up the words that belong to specialist registers. It is usually very easy to identify the profession or field of activity, but encourage students to explore the words they are unfamiliar with.

Answers

a. *The law. **Deem** is a formal word which means **believe; null and void** is a legal term which means **invalid; aforesaid** is a legal term which means **that has been mentioned before.***

b. *The Church. This is the beginning of the Lord's Prayer.* **Art, thy** *and* **trespass** *are archaic.*

c. *Tennis.* **Serve, passing shot, volley, lob** *and* **smash** *are all tennis shots.*

d. *Cooking.* **Marinade, sauté, dice, stock, seasoning** *and* **garnish** *are all to do with cooking.*

e. *Journalese. This is an example of the compact style of headlines.* **The Yard** *is* **Scotland Yard,** *the headquarters of the Criminal Investigation Department;* **to probe** *is used in headlines instead of* **to investigate;** **riddle** *is used instead of* **mystery;** **tot** *is used instead of* **child. Death plunge tot** *is an example of a build-up of nouns to convey a message as compactly as possible. You need to start at the end to decipher it. A child fell to its death.*

f. *Poetry.* **O'er** *is poetic for* **over;** **vale** *is poetic for* **valley.** *These are the first two lines of Wordsworth's 'Daffodils': I wandered lonely as a cloud.*

g. *Horse racing.* **Odds-on favourite** *is a betting term, which means this horse is expected to win;* **the going** *means* **the condition of the ground;** **a filly** *is* **a young female horse.**

h. *Medical profession.* **A cardiac arrest** *is* **a heart attack; a coronary** *is* **a blood clot** *which prevents blood from flowing to the heart.*

i. *Computing.* **A bit** *is the number of items* **a chip** *can deal with at one go.* **K** *stands for* **a thousand.** *This computer can hold* **64,000 bits** *of information in its memory.* **VDU** *means* **visual display unit.** **Disks** *are the means of programming a computer or storing information.*

– Ask students if they know any specialized language from another profession or field of activity. They might know some terms from other sports such as football, skiing, rugby or athletics, or some aviation terminology, for example.

● Listening   (SB 99)

T.22a-b

– Introduction: Ask students what they know about the geography of Britain, and encourage those who have visited Britain to talk about their travels. If you know some parts of Britain well, you could tell the class about them.

1 Students listen to the five people describing where they are from, and take notes under the four headings. They might be able to guess where they are from using the information given; it is unlikely that they will recognize the regional accents, as this is a very difficult thing to do in a foreign language.

Answers

1 *He comes form a large town on a river, and the town used to have an important ship building industry. The town is divided into the West End, where the posh people come from and where the university is, and the poorer East End. He says that people in the East End were rough but friendly. He gives a word from the local dialect,* **drich,** *which means (very) damp.*

This accent pronounces the **r** *which is silent in standard English, and rolls the* **r.** *Listen to the word* **world.**

/aʊ/ is pronounced /uː/, for example **down.**

There is a sound in this dialect which is similar to the way **ch** *is pronounced in German. This sound is heard in the word* **drich.** *Another example is* **loch.**

2 *He comes from a large city which has a port. The city is near Wales. There are several famous landmarks. It is a depressed area because there is a lot of unemployment. The local accent is called Scouse, and it sounds as though people talk through their noses.*

/ɜː/ is pronounced /eə/, for example, **Mersey** *and* **bird.**

Many vowel sounds are lengthened, for example, **large, landmarks** *and* **bird.** *The* **l** *sound is very strong, for example* **locally.**

3 *There are two parts to where he comes from, firstly the moors, which are bleak and wild, and secondly the lush green countryside. The area is very wet, with mists coming in from the sea. The people are warm but not very welcoming to those who come from different parts, so presumably they are warm towards each other! They don't like rushing things.*

Vowel sounds are elongated and slurred in this accent, for example **parts, howling.**

Final consonant sounds are often lost, for example **howling, go(t), li(ke).** *There are many grammatical features, for example* **there be** *and* **we be.**

4 *He comes from a very big county, which has hills, dales, moors and rugged coastline. There used to be a lot of industry, but not so much now. The people have a reputation for being both warm and suspicious of 'comers-in'. The weather is mixed. The word* **the** *is often not pronounced.*

In this accent, /ʌ/ is pronounced /ʊ/, for example **rugged** *and* **comer-in.** */ɑː/ is pronounced like a long /æ/ sound, for example* **hearted.** *There are certain dialect words, for example* **owt** *for* **anything,** *and* **nowt** *for nothing.*

5 *She lives in a town that has a large metal bridge over a river called the Tyne. There are a lot of coal mines. Many people emigrate because the weather is so bad. People from this area are called Geordies. Instead of saying going home, people say* **gannin 'yem.**

In this accent, /eɪ/ is pronounced /ɪə/, for example **famous** *and* **main.** */əʊ/ is pronounced /ʊə/, for example* **most** *and* **know.**

– Students hear the same five people saying where they are from, and they put the numbers 1–5 on the correct place on the map. For the answers, see the map below.

3 Answers

Birmingham d	*Cambridge e*
Manchester b	*Oxford f*
Nottingham c	*Bristol h*
Cardiff g	*Bournemouth i*
Glasgow a	*Belfast j*

4 Discuss these questions as a class. Don't expect too much knowledge from your class. It should be worthwhile, however, for students to know something about the geography of Britain.

Answers

See the map for the location of the places. The West Country consists of the counties of Cornwall, Somerset, Devon and Dorset. They are mainly rural areas of much beauty, with sandy beaches and rugged cliffs.
East Anglia is a flat, rich farming area.
Londonderry is a county in Northern Ireland.
The Pennines are a mountain chain running from the Midlands to northern England. They are known as the backbone of England.
The Highlands of Scotland are a rugged area of great natural beauty including Britain's highest mountain, Ben Nevis, and Loch Ness, famous for its monster.

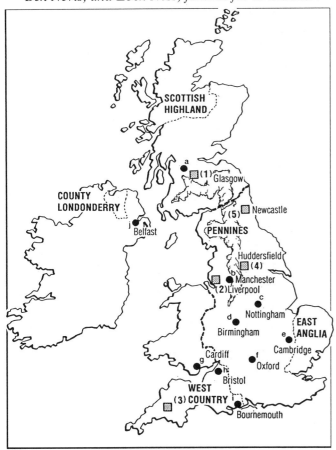

▶ **Language focus** (SB 103 TB 00)

● **Vocabulary 2** (SB 100)

Geographical expressions (SB 100)

– Answer questions a – j in pairs, then k – m as a class. Questions l and m need to be answered very carefully, as giving precise directions is quite difficult. Students could then work in pairs to ask each other similar questions to those in l and m. In questions k to m, point out to students that distances and directions are by road.

Answers

a. *on*
b. *off*
c. *midway*
d. *of*
e. *inland*
f. *to*
g. *at (Canterbury is seen as the whole place. Exactly where in Canterbury doesn't matter. In, however, would also be acceptable.)*
h. *in*
i. *How long does it take to get from Dover to Ostend by ferry?*
j. *How long does it take to get from Dover to Calais by hovercraft?*
k. *8 miles*
l. *Head north out of Deal on the A258 as far as Sandwich. Take the ring road around Sandwich, and then take the A257 westwards as far as Canterbury. Then you need the A290 heading north out of Canterbury, which takes you to Whitstable. You can either take the coast road out of Folkestone, which is the A20 to Dover, or you can head out of Folkestone on the A260 for a mile or so, then take a right onto the B2060. Cross over the main Dover – Canterbury road, and take the A256, which goes all the way to Sandwich. Go out of Hythe on the B2065 crossing over the M20 and under the A20. This road joins the A2. Follow signposts to Canterbury. Take the A28 out of Canterbury heading northeast, and after a mile or so take a left onto the A291, which takes you to Herne Bay.*
m. *Sandwich is seven miles north-west of Deal. Dover is eight miles south-west of Deal. Margate is sixteen miles north-east of Canterbury. Folkestone is about fifteen miles south-east of Canterbury.*
n. *Tolis is not very far from Folkestone.*
o. *It's nine miles in a straight line – the road may wiggle, and so be more than nine miles.*

● Discussion (SB 101)

Home sweet home (SB 101)

- Introduction: Ask students what they understand by 'Home sweet home'. Explain that these words often used to be embroidered and hung on the wall of a home, and they mean that home is the nicest place to be.

- Answer questions 1 – 3 in small groups, then question 4 as a class. A lively, light-hearted discussion should ensue, as national and regional prejudices exist in every country.

- Vocabulary: *posh* means in a sophisticated way; *sissies* are cowardly people; *yokels* are country fools.

LANGUAGE STUDY (SB 102)

1 Relative clauses (SB 102)

- If you think your students need some background information on defining and non-defining relative clauses before beginning this Language study, do Exercise 1 of Unit 9 in the Workbook first.

  There are four exercises in this Language study. You might want to divide them up, perhaps doing question 4 in a later session.

- Ask students to read the Grammar section on relative clauses for homework before starting these exercises.

- In pairs, students decide if sentences a – d contain examples of defining or non-defining relative clauses.

Answers

a. . . . *who looks just like you* is defining.
b. . . . *which is a name* is non-defining.
   . . . *I've never heard before* is defining.
c. . . . *that organizes adventure holidays* is defining.
d. . . . *she was talking to* is defining.
   . . . *which sounded very interesting* is non-defining.

▶ **Grammar reference:** (SB 142)

Practice (SB 102)

Answers

1 a. *All you need to do is contact the police, who'll come immediately.*
  b. *Someone (that) I really admire is Jimmy Savile, who spends all his time raising money for charities that/which care for children.* (**That/which care for children** must be defining, as not all charities care for children, only some of them.)

c. *Last night I went to a party, which was unusual for me* (**which** refers to the whole idea of going to a party) *because I don't usually go to them. I met Alison, who I work with, and she introduced me to her husband, who I had never met before.* (**who I had never met before** is non-defining – she can only have one husband.)

2 a. *The area of Britain my family most likes to visit on holiday is Devon, which is in the south-west of England, and where the weather is usually warm and sunny in summer.*
  b. *We usually stay in a hotel that/which is run by a lovely Italian lady, whose English is almost indecipherable. There are signs in the hotel (that/which) nobody can understand, which doesn't seem to matter, because everything runs very smoothly. The hotel is near the beach that has the highest tide in England.*
  c. *Unfortunately, my children, who usually eat anything that is put in front of them, aren't terribly fond of the food that/which is served there. This is because the people who prepare the food, most of which is Italian, use too many herbs and spices for their liking. Everything they cook is rather rich, which suits my wife and me perfectly.*
  d. *Also, the meal times are rather late for the children. They are used to eating at 5.30, which is when they are hungry after playing all day, but the restaurant doesn't open until 7.00.*
  e. *That is one of the reasons (why) we decided to cater for ourselves this year. We stayed in a cottage we saw advertised in the national press. The lady whose cottage we rented is often abroad on business, which is why she lets it out most of the year.*
  f. *It was one of the nicest cottages we have ever stayed at, and of course, Devon is lovely. It is an area of England that is rich in history, and which offers great hospitality to its visitors.*

3 Read the introduction as a class. Students decide which of the sentences can be joined using both patterns, or whether only one is appropriate.

Answers

a. **The man you were talking to** sounds best.
b. **That's the man I play tennis with** sounds best.
c. **I'll give you the address you should write** to sounds best.
d. *Both patterns are possible.*
e. *Both patterns are possible.*
f. **He was expressing political views I couldn't agree with** sounds best.
g. **Peter is a colleague whose loyalty you can always count on** sounds best.
h. **. . . a disease, from which she suffered for the rest of her life** sounds best.

- There are four exercises in the Workbook to practise relative clauses.

2 Participles   (SB 103)

– Read the introduction as a class. Students re-read the extracts from the three autobiographies and find examples of participles. Don't let this go on too long – four or five minutes should be ample. It is interesting for students to see examples of participles in context, but it is also important that they should practise them.

Answers

a revolving table (line 4)
The fruit shop on the corner facing the Bridge (line 7)
arranged pyramids (line 9)
coloured bus tickets (line 17)
flower-girls . . . making boutonnières (line 20)
. . . fingers manipulating tinsel and quivering fern (line 21)
freshly watered roses (line 22)
children escorting toy windmills (line 24)
hands massaging the crops (line 37)
roads rutted by hooves (line 40)
abetted by levers and pulleys (line 44)
motor-car came coughing up the road (line 53)
Chickens and dogs . . . falling demented (line 56)
old folk . . . faced by speeds (line 57)
My father was somewhere . . . painting signs (line 65)
We looked down the streets . . . hoping we'd see Bird (line 66)

– Students read the Grammar section for homework, or in class, as it is not very long.

▶ **Grammar reference:**   (SB 143)

Practice
Answers

1 a. *employed*
 b. *employing*
 c. *saying*
 d. *missing . . . said*
 e. *written*
 f. *writing*
 g. *wanted*
 h. *wanting*
 i. *feeling*
 j. *felt/seen*
 k. *Seeing*
 l. *Seen*

2 The problem is that the subject of the main clause must also be the subject of the participle clause.

 a. *She gazed with awe at the mountain which rose majestically . . .*
 b. *As I walked along the beach, I noticed that the sea looked warm and inviting.*

 c. *I bought the painting, believed to be at least two hundred years old, and hung it in my living room.*
 d. *This is in fact possible, and means that she loosened his tie. If he did it, the sentence should be As he loosened his tie, she noticed . . .*

REVISION   (SB 103)

Nouns in groups   (SB 103)

– Read the introduction on the three common patterns when nouns are put together. Although the rules for this area of the language are complex, students often manage to 'feel' what is correct.

Practice   (SB 104)

– Students re-read the three extracts to find examples of the three patterns. Don't let this go on too long – about five minutes should be enough.

Answers

1 a. *a thousand years' life (line 31)*
  her day's pay (line 69)

 b. *a galaxy of colour (line 8)*
  pyramids of oranges (line 9)
  the London of my childhood (line 13)
  memories of Lambeth (line 14)
  the corner of Westminster Bridge (line 19)
  the last days of the village (line 29)
  the end of a thousand years' life (line 31)
  handful of years (line 34)
  a world of silence (line 36)
  a world of hard work (line 36)
  the rhythm of our days (line 47)
  the limit of our movements (line 48)
  the size of our world (line 50)
  the scream of the horse (line 52)
  a bag of groceries (line 68)

 c. *tram-cars (line 2)*
  music halls (line 7)
  horse-bus (line 16)
  lilac-trees (line 16)
  flower-girls (line 19)
  toy windmills (line 24)
  penny steamers (line 26)
  Cotswold valley (line 32)
  motor car (line 53)
  motor-bikes (line 59)
  bus fare (line 70)
  World Heavyweight Champion (line 80)
  cardboard (line 98)
  Sunday School (line 101)

2 a. *my parents' advice*
   b. *blood test*
   c. *a bottle of wine*
   d. *a wine bottle*
   e. *government's decision/decision of the government*
   f. *car keys*
   g. *announcement of the disaster*
   h. *teacher's salary*
   i. *night's sleep*
   j. *Prince of Wales' Theatre*
   k. *sister-in-law's farm*
   l. *Mr Thomas's shop*
   m. *back of the car*
   n. *arrival of the Queen/Queen's arrival*
   o. *adventure stories/war films*
   p. *village post office*
   q. *yesterday's newspaper*
   r. *lamb's wool*
   s. *leg of lamb*
   t. *lamb chop*

EXTRA IDEAS

– You could find extracts from other biographies or autobiographies for further reading material, choosing people that you think your class would be interested in.

– Ask students to deliver talks on the subject of their background or that of their parents or grandparents. People generally are very curious about each other, and it is very interesting to hear about other people's upbringing. The writing activity in the unit, where students are invited to describe the sights and smells of their childhood, often produces some fascinating descriptions, and you could ask students to read out loud what they have written.

– For listening material, you could ask an English-speaking friend to make a tape similar to the one in the unit where five people talk about where they are from.

This would be a good opportunity to invite an English-speaking colleague into your class as a guest speaker to talk on the same subject.

– There are often documentaries on British television that could fit the wide-embracing topic of a sense of place.

UNIT 10

Them and Us

OVERVIEW OF THE UNIT

– There are several themes in this unit – the class system in England, newspaper gossip columns, the ethics of journalism, and the Royal Family. There is an article about a wealthy hedonist who spends his year on the social circuit, and an interview with Nigel Dempster, who writes the gossip column for the *Daily Mail*.

– Formal and informal speech is examined, and there is a second focus on ways of adding emphasis. This was first dealt with in Unit 5.

NOTES ON THE LANGUAGE INPUT

Inversion to express emphasis

Work on this area is mainly for recognition purposes, though students may choose to experiment with it in their writing. They should beware of overusing this device, as it can sound cumbersome and bombastic. Inversion presents students with few problems, other than those of *sounding* emphatic when they choose to use an emphatic structure when speaking.

Formal and informal language

It is very difficult to be precise about what makes an item of language more or less formal or more or less informal. Native speakers (in all languages) have an instinctive feel for this based on their life-long exposure to the language, but we suspect that this does not easily transfer to the learner of a foreign language. By and large, students are exposed to and encouraged to produce a neutral style of language, unmarked for formality and appropriate in most situations. It must be said that most language is unmarked in terms of style – bread, chair, car, go, orange, letter, cut, the Present Perfect etc., have no stylistic value at all.

It is perhaps when writing that students feel the need to be on their best linguistic behaviour. For those students who need to write letters in English, there are many conventions and formulae that need to be learnt. Generally speaking, the longer an item is, the more formal it is. Phrasal verbs are avoided where possible, and words of Latin origin are preferred. Modal verbs of ability and obligation might be expressed with **able to** or **obliged to**. Formal letters tend to be more tactful and respectful, and accusations and requests are expressed obliquely. There are two exercises in the Workbook which practise formal and informal language further.

Adverb and verb collocation
Adverb and adjective collocation

Combinations such as **sincerely believe** and **utterly determined** are practised in the first vocabulary exercise. Sometimes there is a logical link which explains why some combinations are possible, for example, **deeply** goes with adjectives that express a feeling.

deeply disappointed
deeply moved

However, more often than not, there is no explanation as to why certain words collocate. We usually say **totally convinced**, but not **totally upset**, **absolutely furious** but not **completely furious**. This can be very frustrating for the learner, but with no clear rules there are no short cuts and the only advice is to learn common collocations.

NOTES ON THE UNIT
● Discussion   (SB 105)

– Ask students if they can make such inferences, albeit over-generalizations, about people in their country from the newspaper they read, the car they drive, their favourite sports, etc.

– Students work in small groups to discuss which social class they associate the newspapers etc. with.

The Times was traditionally read by top people. The *Sun* is the most popular newspaper, most renowned because it has a topless girl on page 3. The *Sporting Life* is all about horse racing, and so has associations with the upper class and the betting fraternity; the *News of the World* is a Sunday newspaper that reports mainly scandal and sensation. *Country Life* is a glossy magazine which advertises very expensive homes and farmland, discusses farming matters and society occasions.

Football doesn't really belong to any particular class. Horse racing is known as the sport of kings, who often breed horses, but of course, people from all classes like betting on horses. Pigeon racing, bowls and darts are probably associated with working classes. There is a tradition of rowing at public schools and universities, and Henley, an annual rowing regatta, attracts many 'champagne-drinking blazers and boater hats'. Fox hunting is traditionally enjoyed by the landed classes, as is pheasant shooting, but shooting rabbits or pigeons may be enjoyed by anyone. Fishing is the most popular sport in Britain, but fishing for salmon is probably quite expensive.

Pimms is quite an exotic drink, served in a tall glass with lots of fruit. Gin and tonic is probably more associated with upper classes, whilst bitter (beer) is common pub fare. Holiday camps in Britain used to be cheap, popular resorts until package holidays brought down the price of holidays abroad. Tropical islands are a long way from Britain, so are expensive to reach.

Range Rovers are popular with country people who need to travel off the road. BMWs are quite expensive. The Ford Escort is the most popular car in Britain.

Ballet and the opera are traditionally enjoyed by middle and upper classes. Gentlemen's clubs are expensive and exclusive. A working man's club is what it says. Bingo (called Lotto in the U.S.A.) is a very popular working class game in some parts of the country.

– The pictures show (right, top to bottom) skiing, darts, a holiday camp 'red coat', (centre) fox hunting, (left top) bingo, (bottom) horse racing spectators.

● Reading (SB 106)

Pre-reading task (SB 106)

The idle rich

– Introduction: Ask your class what they would do if they didn't have to work. How would they fill their time? Where would they go at different times of the year?

– Students read the introduction to the article about Rupert Deen, and the five letters written in reaction to the article.

A relic from the age of Wooster

Bertie Wooster is the creation of P G Wodehouse in books written in the 1920s and 30s. Bertie Wooster was a gentleman of leisure whose life was taken up in idle pursuit. He was something of a fool whose life was organized by his gentleman's gentleman, Jeeves.

Answers

1 *The first letter attacks the life style of people such as Rupert Deen, who the writer describes as a scrounger (a person who tries to get things without working for them.)*
   The second letter is in favour of the article because it was light-hearted, and in favour of Rupert Deen because he does what all of us would do (according to the writer of the letter) if we could afford it.

   The third letter attacks the article because there are many other issues which could have been addressed in the newspaper, and attacks Rupert Deen because he is 'useless'.

   The fourth letter is ultimately in favour of the article because it is 'a salutary lesson to us all' to know that there are such people as Rupert Deen in the world, people of extreme right-wing opinions.

   The last letter thinks that Polly Toynbee didn't realize that she was 'having her leg pulled' in the interview, and that Rupert Deen was telling her what she wanted to hear to write an attack on people such as him in a left-of-centre newspaper.

2 *It is difficult to separate fact and opinion. He obviously doesn't work very much, or not at all. He holds extreme right-wing views, according to the writer of the fourth letter. Anything else that we learn is mainly opinion. Polly Toynbee calls him a wealthy hedonist; the writer of the first letter thinks he should be prosecuted; the writer of the second letter quite warms to him; the writer of the third letter thinks he is useless; the writer of the fourth letter is appalled that such people exist and describes his political views as grotesque.*

3 Students work in pairs to decide what they would like to find out about Rupert Deen when they read the article. Make sure that their questions are well-formed.

Reading and inferring (SB 107)

– The article is quite long, but in fact it is extremely easy to read, with few problems of vocabulary or complex ideas.

– Ask students to take it in turns to read it aloud, discussing vocabulary and content as you go through. Students can then discuss the questions in pairs and re-read the article as necessary.

> A gentleman's gentleman (line 24) is a sort of butler. It sounds very anachronistic. A mews house (35) in London is a converted stable from Victorian or pre-Victorian days. They are often small, but very pretty. Rupert Bear (43) is a character from a children's story, and the nickname 'Bear' sounds very cuddly. In line 57, Rupert Deen talks about completing his levee. This is not a common expression – he means he finishes getting washed and dressed.

– Ask students to answer some of the questions in small groups, and discuss others as a class. Questions 10 – 12 lend themselves to class discussion.

Answers

1 *She is a serious journalist writing for a serious newspaper. The Guardian is a left-of-centre newspaper, and she probably wanted to expose the lives of such idle rich people.*
2 *A personal butler.*
  Margaret washes and cleans for him.
3 *Probably, but we don't know.*
4 *Amanda is described as a somewhat peripheral character. Polly Toynbee obviously didn't like her. She giggles. 'A beautiful blond girl friend' is mock imitation of the style of popular newspapers. She has nothing of any intelligence to add to the interview apart from* **Really!** *and* **Honestly!** *Polly Toynbee thinks that the nickname Bear is very silly.*
5 *Lunchtime, when twice a week he has to discuss business. There isn't really a busy part of his day.*
6 *It isn't strenuous. It is more like gambling than work.*
7 *It wasn't very academic, but it taught him about the world. It sounds as though he learnt how to make money through investments, survive socially and get on with women.*
8 *May, the south of France; Ascot (a prestigious horse race) and Wimbledon (tennis) in June; July, more horse races and a golf championship; August, the (cricket) test match between England and a touring side; after the Glorious Twelfth (of August, when grouse shooting is allowed) he shoots grouse; then he goes back to the south of France; he goes to the Arc de Triomphe horse race in Paris in early October, then drives back to England in time to shoot pheasants, visiting stud farms in Normandy en route. In December he shoots a lot. During the rest of the year he travels to exotic countries.*
9 *He may qualify as a male; educated; contributing to society; employing people indirectly.*
10 *He was probably pulling Polly Toynbee's leg a little, and exaggerating the leisureliness of his*

life-style to annoy the serious journalist. In the final column especially he seems to express views that are designed to shock.
However, no doubt many of the facts of his life and how he fills his time are true.
11 *As a selfish, self-opinionated, undeserving possessor of great wealth, with a most undesirable set of political values.*
12 *She would probably most sympathize with the fourth. (In our opinion, the fourth and the fifth are most appropriate.)*

What do you think? (SB 107)

– Answer the 'What do you think?' questions as a class.

Answers

The first two questions have no set answers.

3 *He is easy-going, nothing bothers him very much. He doesn't seem terribly sincere from the interview. He is a reactionary rather than radical in that his political views are extremely right-wing. We have no way of knowing whether he belongs to the aristocracy. He is sporting in that he likes a lot of sport. He doesn't appear to be ambitious, in that he has no real job and nothing that he is striving to achieve. We have no reason to suppose that he is either generous or ungenerous, neither artistic or unartistic. He appears to have been supercilious in his attitude to the interviewer. He is in no way a liberal. As for whether he is charming, some would say no and others would say yes.*

▶ **Language focus** (SB 112 TB 82)

● **Vocabulary 1** (SB 108)

1 Adverb and verb collocations (SB 108)

> Students need to approach this exercise and the next with a certain caution. As we explained in the 'Notes on the language input', there is sometimes a logical link which explains the collocation, for example, **sincerely believe** and **distinctly remember**.
>
> However, in their frustration, students might begin to guess wildly, and want an explanation as to why they can't say *strongly refuse or *totally refuse. Sometimes it can be difficult for the teacher to say whether a combination is possible or not. The obvious collocation with **deny** is **categorically**, but **completely** and **totally** are also possible. The best advice is to accept (and encourage students to learn) only the common collocations.

a. *sincerely/firmly*
b. *sincerely*
c. *categorically*
d. *freely*
e. *deeply*
f. *sincerely/seriously*
g. *distinctly*
h. *totally/completely*
i. *totally/categorically*
j. *entirely/absolutely/ completely/totally*
k. *deeply/greatly*
l. *fully/totally*
m. *totally/strongly*
n. *strongly/seriously*

2 Adverb and adjective collocations (SB 109)

– Read the introduction as a class.

1 Students work in pairs to match an adverb and an adjective.

Answers
bitterly disappointed
deeply moved
perfectly simple
deeply disturbed
fully informed
deeply offended

2 Before beginning question 2, make sure students know the difference between gradable and limit adjectives. This is quite a difficult concept, and it is not always possible to decide whether an adjective is one or the other. (Some adjectives, such as **beautiful**, can be both.) Write the adjective **hot** on the board, and ask students if we can say **very hot**. (The answer, of course, is yes.) Ask students if they know a word that means very hot. The answer is **boiling**. Ask if we can say **very boiling**. The answer is no. Ask students why. They might say that it doesn't sound right, which is a good answer, and you can now explain the difference between gradable and limit adjectives. Explain that to make a limit adjective stronger, we need an extreme adverb, so we can say **absolutely boiling**.

Put the following gradable adjectives on the board, and ask students to think of their limit equivalent.

clever (brilliant)
funny (hilarious)
valuable (priceless)
big (vast, huge, enormous)
dirty (filthy)
angry (furious)
frightened (terrified, petrified)

– Read the introduction to question 2. Students work in pairs to match an adverb and an adjective.

Answers
greatly relieved
terribly important
terribly simple
terribly/greatly annoyed
greatly/terribly impressed
terribly disappointed
greatly/terribly offended

3 Again, there is very little logic that explains why certain combinations are possible. You can tell students that **absolutely** can go with nearly all limit adjectives, but other collocations must be learnt.

Remember that **quite** is a difficult adverb. It can go with limit adjectives and means to *an extreme degree*. It can also go with gradable adjectives and what it means depends on how it is said.

It's quite 'good. (weak **quite**, stressed **good**)
This is positive. *I like it.*

It's 'quite good. (stressed **quite**, weak **good**)
This is negative. *It's all right, but not wonderful.*

It's 'quite 'good. (equal stress)
This is neutral. *It's moderately good.*

Answers
absolutely delighted
absolutely/utterly/quite disgusted
absolutely/totally/utterly/quite convinced
absolutely/utterly appalled
absolutely/utterly/quite determined
absolutely/totally/quite obvious
absolutely/utterly amazed
totally/quite untrue

Practice (SB 109)

– Students work in pairs to devise some questions which will elicit the use of one of the collocations. This is a contrived activity, so don't worry if some of the questions and answers sound a little unnatural.

– There are two exercises in the Workbook that practise the collocations in this vocabulary exercise.

● Writing and speaking (SB 109)

T.23

– Writing activities test accuracy rather than fluency, because the written word does not tolerate error as the spoken language does. When students come to give their talk, you could let them read what they have written, or allow them notes, so they have to reconstruct their argument as they speak. It is probably best to do questions 1 and 2 in class, and then ask students to write their speech for homework. You can then correct it before it is read out to the rest of the class. This way, students should have a certain confidence that what they are saying is correct English.

1 Look again at the ways of adding emphasis on page 58 of Unit 5.

2 The tape will set the tone for the exercise. Students might groan at the prospect of having to make a formal speech in front of their colleagues,

but the activity should be good fun and light-hearted, and the speech on tape should raise a few laughs. It contains examples of many of the devices for adding emphasis, including the use of intensifying adverbs.

Answers

Never before has this country faced . . .
what is needed is courage . . .
Should we fail . . .
absolutely disastrous . . .
It is at moments such as these that . . .
What we must all realize is that . . .
on no account and in no circumstances . . .
Were we to act as they suggest . . .
not only that I was defeated, but also that . . .

3 Encourage students to write a speech on a topic shown, or of their own choice if they want.

4 Depending on the number of students in your class, you might want to spread out the speeches over a number of lessons. On the other hand, each speech will probably not last more than three or four minutes, and to have all the speeches at the same time would give the activity a certain momentum.

● Listening   (SB 110)

T.24

- Introduction: Take in some copies of newspapers that have a gossip column, ideally including the *Daily Mail*. This could be done with papers in your students' own language if you are teaching outside Britain. Students scan the articles to see who is being talked about and what they are supposed to have done. Ask students what the tone of the articles seems to be. Often they are cloyingly sycophantic.

Pre-listening task   (SB 110)

- Students discuss the questions in the pre-listening task in small groups. Get feedback on the questions that seem to interest your class.

Listening for information   (SB 111)

- Students listen to the interview and answer the questions.

Answers

1 *He answers it in that he says the main aim is informing readers, but he doesn't actually say whether he thinks that there is a serious purpose behind this. He says that entertaining readers is of secondary importance.*

2 *He seems to suggest that he thinks his column has a serious purpose, and this would add to his own sense of self-importance. However, it is hard to believe that people read his column to obtain facts about what happens in places of power and privilege.*

3 *Something silly, for example, getting drunk at a party. Something sexual, for example, having an affair with a married person. Financial misdemeanours, for example, swindling your company. Treating someone badly, for example, sacking an employee unjustly.*

4 *He is extremely scornful, perhaps because he writes for a rival newspaper. (In fact, he began writing his gossip column for the Express, and then left to join the Mail.)*

5 *He can choose who to write about, and what to write about them (except that, according to Dempster, it must be true). He says that people do not usually enjoy being in his column.*

The word subject makes his study of the people he writes about sound scientific, and hence, perhaps, more accurate.

6 *He says that the basic ingredient for gossip is a homogeneous society, that is, quite a small society that is mainly united and knows each other. If you don't know, or haven't heard of, the people that the gossip is about, you won't be interested in it.*

7 *By the people who move in Royal circles, such as detectives and staff.*

8 *He would appear to be a loyal supporter of the Royals. He calls the Queen Mother great, and is proud of the fact that he knows the Queen speaks French extremely well. On the other hand, he says that they have a duty to be doing something every day, as they lead rich and gilded lives.*

9 *He is contemptuous of it, saying that it is all invention.*

What do you think?   (SB 111)

- Answer the 'What do you think?' questions as a class. A lively discussion should ensue.

▶ Language focus   (SB 113, TB 82)

● Vocabulary 2   (SB 112)
Synonyms in context   (SB 112)

1 Students work in pairs to fill the gaps with a word with a similar meaning to the one in italics. This exercise is best done with lexicons.

Answers

a. *irritates/bugs (slang)*
b. *quarrelling/arguing/
   bickering*
c. *raid/assault*
d. *relieved*
e. *summit/peak*
f. *withdrew*
g. *stunned*
h. *crafty/sly/sneaky*

2 This exercise takes a long time to do well. You might choose to start it in class and ask students to finish it for homework, or do it over two sessions.

Answers

a. *antiquated practices/ideas
   antique furniture
   current situation/method/rate
   up-to-date news*
b. *open-minded person/attitude
   impartial advice/observer
   liberal attitude
   bigoted person
   prejudiced person/information
   biased person/opinion*
c. *impeccable taste/behaviour
   faultless performance
   immaculate white dress/behaviour
   flawed argument
   faulty machine
   second-rate actor/shop*
d. *trivial information/matter
   petty crime/detail
   insignificant minority
   essential qualifications
   urgent problem
   vital information/importance*

LANGUAGE STUDY (SB 112)

1 Inversion to express emphasis (SB 112)

– Read the introduction and the examples of sentences with inversion as a class. Ask a student to read out loud the five sentences containing an inversion, and check that they sound emphatic!

– Students read the Grammar section for homework or in class, as it is not very long.

▶ **Grammar reference:** (SB 144)

Practice (SB 112)

– Students work in pairs to transform the sentences.

Answers

a. *Never will the Director give in to public pressure.*
b. *No sooner had the meeting started than fighting broke out in the audience.*

c. *Not for one moment did Henry suspect his brother of complicity in the crime.*
d. *Never in all my life have I been so surprised.*
e. *Nowhere will you find craftsmanship of such quality.*
f. *Never again will I allow such practices to take place.*
g. *Only when he was certain of his results did he announce his discovery to the world.*
h. *Only after it has matured for ten years is good whisky ready for consumption.*
i. *Not only has this government deceived the public, (but) it has deceived itself.*
j. *In no circumstances should this door be left open.*
k. *Not only are the values of our society at risk, but the very survival of the nation is threatened.*
l. *Never before has this country been so threatened.*
m. *Rarely are artists appreciated while they are still alive.*
n. *Little do children realize that their world of innocence soon disappears.*
o. *At no time did I intend to deceive you.*
p. *Were I ever to tell you a lie, I wouldn't be able to look you in the eye.*
q. *Not only do I respect her opinions, (but) I admire her character greatly as well.*
r. *Should you require any further information, don't hesitate to contact me.*
s. *Not since I was at university have I had to study so hard.*
t. *Had I not witnessed the experiment with my own eyes, I would never have believed it could be done.*
   Or
   If I hadn't witnessed the experiment with my own eyes, never would I have believed it could be done.

– There are three exercises in the Workbook that practise inversions further.

2 Formal and informal language (SB 113)

1 Students work in pairs to correct the mistakes of style.

Answers

a. *the debate about the state of the National . . .
   the Government narrowly won it.
   two Members of Parliament disagreed/had a
   difference of opinion . . .
   The Honourable Member for East Croydon
   considered/thought that . . .
   accused the Prime Minister of misleading the
   House.*
b. *I don't want to talk about this any more.
   tidy your room right now . . .
   no way I'll take you to the cinema, as I said I
   would.*

c. *We have gathered here today to witness . . .*
   James, will you take Anne as your . . .
   I will.
d. *Consequently, the number of chickens born has increased considerably.*

---

2 It is very difficult to be precise regarding what makes an item of language more or less formal. See the Notes on language input at the beginning of this unit of the Teacher's Book.
Phrasal verbs are often more informal – **go on** versus **happen**.
Anglo-Saxon words are less formal than their Latinate equivalents – **row** versus **argument**; **reckon** versus **consider**; **talk** versus **negotiate**.
Get is avoided where possible.
Formal language contains more complex sentences.

---

3 **Answers**

Dear Ms Denton

Thank you for your letter of 24 May. As I am sure you will appreciate, I am most upset to learn that you were unable to locate my suitcase. As I pointed out in my original letter, the suitcase contained many documents that I require for my work. I have been obliged to contact my publishers to obtain copies of documents that your airline mislaid. Naturally, I will complete the Claim Form, but I find it difficult to estimate the value of the documents. Approximately half of them are irreplaceable.

I trust that in the meantime you continue to look for my case. Should you find it, please contact me immediately.

I look forward to hearing from you.
Yours sincerely
James Burke

4 Students could discuss this in pairs in class to get some ideas together, then write the letter for homework.

– There is a further exercise on formal and informal language in the Workbook.

REVISION (SB 115)

Pronouns – 'one', 'you', and 'they' (SB 115)

– Although students recognize these uses of **you** and **they**, they do not use them freely, perhaps because they translate from their own languages, or because

they prefer to use a personal subject where colloquial English is more vague, or because, having learned not to use **one**, they use the passive.

– Read the introduction as a class.

Practice (SB 115)
Answers
a. *your*
b. *They*
c. *one . . .   one . . .   oneself . . .   one*
d. *you*
e. *You . . .   they . . .   you*
f. *you . . .   you . . .   you*
g. *They*
h. *They . . .   they*
i. *You . . .   you . . .   your*
j. *they . . .   you . . .   your . . .   you/they*

EXTRA IDEAS

– This is a good opportunity for you to examine the styles of different newspapers, by comparing the way they handle the same story. It is not vital to use English language newspapers for this. Select a quality newspaper and one or two popular newspapers, and divide the class into groups.
Put questions on the board such as the following:
What page is the story on?
Is there any bias in the headline?
How much space is the article given?
Are there any photographs?
Are there any quotes?
What angle does the article take?
What detail is given?

– An obvious area for discussion is to compare the class system in different countries and how it manifests itself – is it in education, profession, entertainment, address, possessions such as car or clothes?

– Your class might be interested in having a discussion about the role of the Royal Family. There is a supplementary reading text on page 84 of this Teacher's Book written by Willy Hamilton, an MP who is renowned for his attacks on the Royal Family, and another on page 65 of the Workbook. There are nearly always articles about them in newspapers and magazines.

– You could record an English-speaking friend discussing his/her attitudes towards any of the issues raised in this unit.

AN OPEN LETTER TO
HER MAJESTY QUEEN ELIZABETH II

Your Majesty,

1.   You must surely agree that, by birth and upbringing, by the surroundings in which you live and the company you keep, you cannot possibly understand the feelings and the way of life of the millions of ordinary people it is claimed you keep united in one big happy family. It is a claim you have never contradicted, but in your heart of hearts, deep inside yourself, you know how absurd it is.

2.   You are known to be among the wealthiest women, if not the wealthiest woman, in the world. It is not wealth that has been created by any business acumen of your own, or even of your financial advisers (though they have helped). It is wealth that has been built up by invaluable, fabulous and unique tax concessions granted by Parliament, and never refused by you. You do not even pay taxes on the profits of your private estates at Sandringham and Balmoral. Whatever many of your people believe, you pay no income tax. You receive a refund of any taxes deducted from dividends on investments. You pay no capital gains tax. You pay no death duty. What do you do with it all?

3.   Large numbers of those known as 'your people' share the views I hold – many more than you are led to believe. They regard the *institution* of Monarchy as an instrument used to make respectable to the unthinking and the irrational a social and economic class system which is unfair, divisive and often cruel.

4.   There are still a few people around who think that the divine right of kings lingers, that you still retain some real political power. But whatever else you have – it is not *political* power. The so-called royal prerogatives, the 'right' to appoint your own Prime Minister, the 'right' to dissolve Parliament, are now no more than ritual play-acting.

5.   Meanwhile, you are to be seen at your radiant best at annual high-society horsey events, and, quite frankly, at your most uncomfortable among factory workers, or even children.

6.   I suspect you to be the willing victim of circumstance, that you are suffocated by hoards of sinecured hangers-on. We may not know what any of these are paid or what they do. Questions about their salaries are courteously turned aside. Almost all members of the Royal Households are titled nonentities, drawn, it seems automatically, from one narrow section of the community.

7.   But then your daily round, your common task, furnishes you and yours with even more than you need to ask. Your sense of financial security and well-being is a dream yearned after by millions of your people. They cannot understand why you and your family should be so privileged and they so deprived. They look to you for genuine moral leadership, but do not hear from you or your husband one unequivocal word on the evils of racial prejudice when two million of your subjects in Britain alone are coloured. You encourage cruel blood sports, yet remain President of the Royal Society for the Prevention of Cruelty to Animals.

8.   Many long to hear from you one occasional speech that contains not just colourless, negative clichés, but a forthright and passionate sincerity, a personal conviction.

I remain,
Your wayward subject,
W.W. HAMILTON

UNIT 11

The brain

OVERVIEW OF THE UNIT

– The theme of the brain and its potential runs throughout the unit. There is a short interview with Edward de Bono, who gives an illustration of what he means by lateral thinking, and an interview with Tony Buzan, who has written several books on how to use your brain more effectively. The reading text concerns the problem of defining mental illness.

– In the Language study, there is the second focus on tense usage for fact and non-fact, with exercises on the subjunctive.

NOTES ON THE LANGUAGE INPUT

Hypothesizing about the past, present and future

Tense usage for non-fact was first dealt with in Unit 7, where conditional sentences were examined. In this unit, various other structures which express non-fact are practised, including **wish, if only, look as if, it's time** and **would rather**. Students are carefully guided to perceive the difference between Past Simple forms to refer to real past time and Past Simple forms that hypothesize about the present and future; similarly the Past Perfect which refers to the real past-in-the-past, and the Past Perfect which hypothesizes about the past. If students perceive this difference, then tense usage to express non-fact is quite logical and straightforward – they merely have to work out what is fact, what tense is needed to express this fact, and shift the verb form backwards.

Example

I don't have a job. (Present Simple to express a present fact.)
I wish I had a job. (Past Simple to hypothesize about the present.)

Despite the logic, some students can have a lot of difficulty with this area, so be prepared to re-present the rules and explain as much as necessary.

Tense usage for non-fact is further practised in the writing exercise in the Student's Book, and there are four exercises in the Workbook.

The Present Subjunctive

This form is rare, but nevertheless exists, especially in written English. It is an area of the language that many advanced students have never encountered before – either they have not come across it in their reading and listening, or they have never consciously focused their attention on it. Having been shown how it operates, they can be most unwilling to use it! They can find it most peculiar that a third person singular subject can be followed by a verb stem without -s! It certainly does sound stylized, but it is worth pointing out. Students often feel much happier using **should** to avoid the Present Subjunctive.

NOTES ON THE UNIT
● **Problem solving** (SB 116)

T.25

– Students work in pairs to solve the problems.

Answers

1 *25 (Apple = 7; banana = 8; cherry = 2; pineapple = 3)*
2 *9 (Down 6; up 3; down 5; up 2; down 4; up 1)*
3 *GUJ (The vowels come in alphabetical order in the middle of the sequence, so U is the next vowel. The first letter in the sequence is from the alphabet in alphabetical order but without the vowels. The third letter is the same, beginning with the letter D.)*
4 *60 days (Half the number of men will take the same time to dig half the number of holes.)*

5 *Ant (Ants live in large, complicated nests.)*
6 *Golf (You play with a golf club at a golf club.)*
  Football (You can play another team at football with a football.)
7 *Mourning (The other three are synonyms.)*
8 *Paul (If Paul were telling the truth, then the other two are also telling the truth, so no one is lying. Therefore we know that Paul is one of the people telling a lie. So either Ben or Sam must be telling the truth. But we know that Ben didn't steal the cake, so Ben is also lying, because he agreed with it. Sam is therefore the one telling the truth. He didn't take it, and neither did Ben, so it must have been Paul.)*

Listening and pairwork   (SB 116)

– Read the introduction as a class. If students want to know what lateral thinking is, tell them that they will hear an example of it in the interview.

– Play the introduction and the first part of de Bono's story about the worms up to 'Oh that's strange, there's only two holes'. Students work in pairs to think of possible explanations.

– Listen to de Bono's answer.

– Ask students if they can explain the difference between logical and lateral thinking. Lateral thinking is a method of solving problems by using your imagination to help you think of solutions that are not at first obvious. Logical thinking doesn't place such importance on imagination.

– Students consider the three problems, and try to think of possible explanations.

Answers

1 *The man wants the water because he has the hiccups. The barmaid knows this, so screams to give him a shock, which is said to stop the hiccups.*
2 *They were used to build a snowman when, naturally, there was snow on the ground. The snow has since melted.*
3 *The man is a dwarf. He can only reach the button for the eighth floor.*

These three problems are illustrative of the concept of lateral thinking. A logical answer can be given but it is not totally satisfactory – it doesn't 'feel' right. The answer arrived at by 'lateral' thinking not only explains the situation but feels so right that there can be no other explanation.

In order to perceive the answer in this way your students should have a chance to puzzle out the answer logically. This provides a language fluency opportunity for 'asking questions'. In principle it doesn't really matter whether you force students to use YES/NO questions – a bit unnatural but

---

acceptable as a game – or let them ask open questions. The latter is probably to be preferred as their questions will be natural and by carefully judging how much information to give you can guide them (but not too quickly) towards the solution.

Example

1. **Q.** Where is the bar?
   A. It doesn't matter.
2. **Q.** How are these things connected?
   A. That's the key to the solution.
3. **Q.** Why does he walk up from the eight to the thirteenth floor?
   A. Well, he doesn't need the exercise, that's for sure.

– Such problem solving situations can be very difficult to work out, until you know the answer and then they seem so obvious! You can expect a few groans when you give the solutions.

As an additional puzzle try the following:
My aunt likes coffee but she doesn't like tea.
She likes beer but she doesn't like gin.
She likes swimming but she doesn't like sailing.

Key – your aunt likes any word which includes a double letter (*coffee*, *beer*), in its spelling. You can make up many more examples. When one or more students have understood the key encourage them to give further examples of their own, not to give the key away. This puzzle can be continued off and on for weeks.

NB: don't write the examples down for your students otherwise it is too easy.

● Vocabulary 1   (SB 117)
Idiomatic expressions   (SB 117)

– Read the introduction as a class, and answer the question about the basic difference between the words **mind** and **brain**.

Answer

Mind is abstract; brain is physical.

1 Students work in pairs to find the differences between the words and expressions, using the dictionary entries.

Answers

a. **mindless** *means paying no attention;* **brainless** *means stupid.*
b. **A brainwave** *is a good idea;* **brainwashing** *is a way of forcing a person to change their opinions.*

c. **To have something on the brain** *means to think constantly about it, for example a song;* **to have something on one's mind** *means to have a problem that you can't see an easy solution to.*

d. **To have a good brain** *means to be intelligent;* **to have a good mind to do something** *means to intend firmly to do something.*

e. **To have a brainstorm** *means to be momentarily confused;* **mindblowing** *is a colloquial expression meaning causing great excitement;* **to be out of one's mind** *means to be mad.*

f. **To rack one's brains** *means to try very hard to think of something;* **to pick someone's brains** *means to ask someone to help you with a problem because they know a lot about the subject.*

g. **To be in two minds** *about something means you are uncertain about what to do, especially when you have to choose between two courses of action;* **to know one's own mind** *means you know exactly what you want.*

2 a. *a brainwave*
   b. *picks her brains*
   c. *We're really in two minds about whether*
   d. *out of your mind*
   e. *I've racked my brains*
   f. *mindblowing*

● Reading (SB 118)

– Introduction: Ask your students if they have seen the film *One flew over the cuckoo's nest*, a film which showed the plight of some men in a mental hospital, and the ways in which they either accepted or resisted the hospital regime. Actor Jack Nicholson (photo) played the leading role in this film.

Pre-reading task (SB 118)

– Students work in small groups to think of synonyms for the word mad. This was in fact dealt with in Unit 1!

Answers

insane, deranged, mentally unbalanced *describe the medical condition.*

lunatic, crazy, nuts, berserk *are more informal.*

Scan reading (SB 118)

– Read the introduction as a class. Students read the extract from *Mindwatching* quickly to decide what was the main purpose of the experiment.

Answer

*All are possible answers, but the **main** reason was to show that it is often difficult for psychiatrists to distinguish between the sane and the insane.*

– Students read the extract in more detail, and answer the questions.

Comprehension check (SB 119)

Answers

1 a.	*5 and 6*	g.	*3 and 4*
b.	*8*	h.	*13*
c.	*1*	i.	*12*
d.	*7*	j.	*10*
e.	*2*	k.	*11*
f.	*9*		

– An interesting activity to do at this point is to ask students in pairs to practise reading out loud the second paragraph of the extract. It contains some long words that are notoriously difficult for students to pronounce, for example, **psychiatrist**, **psychology**, **psychiatric**.

– Students work in groups of three to answer questions 2 and 3. This is more of a comprehension exercise than a writing exercise, so don't let it go on too long – a maximum of ten minutes.

What do you think? (SB 120)

– Answer the 'What do you think?' questions as a class.

Vocabulary (SB 120)

– Students work in pairs to match a word with its definition.

Answers

a. *shabby (line 18)*
b. *thud (line 25)*
c. *pseudo (line 38)* /sjuːdəʊ/
d. *bona fide (line 86)* /bəʊnəfaɪdɪ/
e. *at face value (line 88)*
f. *blurred (line 90)*
g. *gullible (line 98)*

▶ Language focus (SB 122, TB 88)

● Listening (SB 120)

T.26

Pre-listening task (SB 120)

– Answer the first two questions as a class. If you don't get much response, ask questions such as the following, or give some information such as the following:

What colour is it? (greyish-pink)
What's the surface like? (It's got lots of ridges and grooves.)

How much does it weigh? (It is fully grown when a person is six years old, and weighs about three pounds/1.4 kilogrammes.)
Do brain cells reproduce as we get older? (Very little. Most of the brain cells are present at birth. The increase in weight comes mainly from growth of the cells.)

The brain works like both a computer and a chemical factory. Brain cells produce electrical signals and send them from cell to cell along pathways called circuits. As in a computer, these electrical circuits receive, process, store and retrieve information. Unlike a computer, however, the brain creates its electrical signals by chemical means. The proper functioning of the brain depends on many complicated chemical substances produced by brain cells.

In simple animals such as worms and insects, the brain consists of small groups of nerve cells. All animals with a backbone have a complicated brain made of many parts. Animals that have an exceptionally well-developed brain include apes, dolphins and whales. Human beings have the most highly-developed brain of all. It consists of billions of interconnected cells, and enables people to use language, solve difficult problems and create works of art.

– Students work in pairs to decide whether they think the statements are true or false. Ask for their opinions before you play the tape.

Listening and checking   (SB 120)

– Students listen to the interview and check the true/false answers.

Answers

1 *False. In practice it is more receptive when we are young, because there is relatively more information to take in. In theory, the brain's potential is such that we could learn more and more the older we get.*
2 *True.*
3 *False. If you continue to stimulate it, it will get better.*
4 *True. Non-use will also make it deteriorate, but this isn't permanent.*
5 *False.*
6 *True.*
7 *False. They don't mention anything about the body becoming top-heavy, but this evolution will certainly not happen soon.*
8 *True. (Students might want to argue that this is false, as this is a hypothesis only.)*

What do you think?   (SB 120)

– Answer the 'What do you think?' questions as a class.

▶ **Language focus**   (SB 123, TB 89)

● Speaking and writing   (SB 121)

– Read the introduction as a class.

– Students work in groups of three to write their story. They usually produce some extremely amusing versions! In frames 9 and 10, it is important to note that the season has changed. He began thinking with the tree in leaf, and continues to think until the autumn!

– Allow adequate time for this activity. It usually takes a class a while to get organized. When they are ready, the groups take it in turns to read out their story.

● Vocabulary 2   (SB 122)
Nouns formed from multi-word verbs (SB 122)

– Read the introduction as a class.

Practice   (SB 122)

– Students work in pairs to fill the gaps. This is quite a difficult exercise, as there is often no logical explanation as to why the noun means what it does.

Answers

1 a. *drawback*   i. *outlook*
  b. *cutbacks*   j. *downfall*
  c. *setback*   k. *breakdown*
  d. *flashbacks*   l. *shake-up*
  e. *outcome*   m. *cover-up*
  f. *blackout*   n. *standby/stand-by*
  g. *outcry*   o. *tip-off*
  h. *handout*

– There is another exercise on nouns formed from multi-word verbs in Unit 12 of the Workbook.

LANGUAGE STUDY   (SB 122)

1 Hypothesizing   (SB 122)

1 Ask students to read the Grammar section on expressing hypothesis for homework before doing this exercise.

Read the introduction as a class. Students look at the sentences, and decide whether the examples of the Past Simple refer to the real past times or not.

Answers

a. *grew – no*
b. *walked – yes*
c. *couldn't – yes*
d. *could – no*
e. *had – yes*
f. *had – no*
g. *Did you fall – yes*
h. *didn't tell – no*
i. *owned – no*
j. *weren't – no*
k. *didn't have to – no*
l. *had to – yes*

All 'no' answers have in common the fact that they are expressing a hypothesis, something which isn't true about the present and future.

2 Students look at the sentences, and decide whether the examples of the Past Perfect refer to the real past-in-the-past or not.

Answers

a. *hadn't said – no*
b. *I'd seen – yes*
c. *Had I realized – no*
d. *had never been invented – no*
e. *hadn't told – yes*
f. *had told – no*
g. *you'd seen – no*
h. *he'd had – yes*

All 'no' answers have in common the fact that they are expressing a hypothesis, something which isn't true about the past.

▶ **Grammar reference:** (SB 144)

Practice (SB 123)

Answers

1 a. *I wish I didn't forget people's names.*
  b. *I wish you didn't live so far from us.*
  c. *If only you wouldn't smoke so much.*
  d. *If only you wouldn't tell lies.*

2 One aim of this question is to show that **would** cannot be used when the subject and object of **wish** are the same.

All possibilities are correct except:

I wish I would remember*
He wishes he would remember*

3 This exercise is in the form of a dialogue. Students should skim through it first to understand the situation and establish tenses.

a. *hadn't come*
b. *have never seen*
c. *was/were*
d. *could*
e. *is*
f. *wouldn't even wash*
g. *was getting*
h. *had been driving*
i. *wanted*
j. *would we have stayed*
k. *went*
l. *will find*
m. *promise*
n. *wasn't/weren't*
o. *would suggest*
p. *went/go*
q. *did*
r. *would stop*
s. *decide/decided*
t. *are*
u. *were/was*
v. *would never decide*

– There are four exercises on hypothesizing in the Workbook.

2 The Present Subjunctive (SB 123)

– Read the introduction as a class. As was said in the 'Notes on the Language Input', students often find the form of the Present Subjunctive most peculiar! Having pointed it out to your students, look out for examples you might come across in further listenings and readings. It is in fact more frequent than might be thought.

– Students read the Grammar section in class, as it is quite short.

▶ **Grammar reference:** (SB 145)

Practice (SB 123)

Answers

a. *She suggested that he study/should study . . .*
b. *He proposed that they finish/should finish . . .*
c. *The captain commanded that the prisoner be taken/should be taken below deck and tied up.*
d. *The waiter recommended that we have/should have the beef.*
e. *The chairperson insisted that the minutes of the meeting be read/should be read.*
f. *It is important that the contract be signed/should be signed . . .*

g. *It is essential that the candidates have/should have . . .*
h. *The Prime Minister requested that a full inquiry take/ should take place.*

– There is a further exercise on the Present Subjunctive in the Workbook.

REVISION   (SB 124)

Informal speech   (SB 124)

1 Students work in pairs to match a line from column A with a line from column B.

Answers

1	*h*	
2	*e*	
3	*j*	
4	*b*	
5	*o*	*chuffed = pleased*
6	*n*	*fiver = five pounds*
		no way = definitely not
7	*k*	*piece of cake = easy*
8	*i*	
9	*a*	*wasn't born yesterday = am intelligent/ experienced*
10	*d*	*blew it = failed*
11	*c*	*bits and bobs = things*
12	*m*	
13	*f*	
14	*g*	
15	*l*	*not half = I agree/exactly*

2 Students work in pairs to write a short dialogue incorporating some examples of informal speech. Monitor this very carefully, as the meanings of the items are very specific, and students often over-generalize them, and try to apply them to situations where they aren't applicable.

EXTRA IDEAS

– Depending on the interests of your students, you might like to do any of the many tests that exist to assess personality, IQ, or work aptitude. Discussing which answer is correct can be very challenging. H.J. Eysenck has written several such books, which are available in Pelican.

– Edward de Bono has written a series of tasks to develop thinking skills, and these can be very stimulating to do with students. They are called *CoRT Thinking*, and are published by Pergamon Press, Oxford.

– You could recommend that they read *One flew over the Cuckoo's Nest* by Ben Kersey.

UNIT 12

The meaning of life

OVERVIEW OF THE UNIT

– There are several themes in this unit – world religions, life after death and the creation of the universe. There is an article about people who have had Near Death Experiences and their glimpse into the possibility of an after life, and an interview with Dr Carl Sagan, the American cosmologist.

– The Revision section in this unit is a revision test of much of the language work in *Headway Advanced*.

NOTES ON THE LANGUAGE INPUT

Nouns with a special meaning in the plural

The first vocabulary exercise in this unit looks at nouns which go with particular uncountable nouns, for example, **a lump of coal**.

The first Language study focuses on those nouns which have a special meaning in the plural, for example, **fruit** as an uncountable noun and **the fruits of her labours**, where fruits means results. Students are often unaware of the alternative meanings of these words.

'They' referring to a singular person

This use has become more common in the attempt to avoid saying only **he** or **he and she**.

The use of '-ever' for emphasis

This is the third exercise on emphatic structures. The others are in Units 5 and 10. Students often recognize structures such as **whatever** etc., but often fail to produce them when appropriate.

In the Workbook, there is more input on nouns and noun phrases, with work on articles, noun collocations, and collective nouns.

NOTES ON THE UNIT

● **Discussion** (SB 125)

We feel that a well-rounded advanced speaker of English should be able to discuss religious topics and understand religious concepts in English. However one's religion is a deeply personal subject and this unit should be handled sensitively. There may even be disputes about 'factual' answers and a range of answers must be allowed for. In particular, watch out for students who do not want to discuss their religion or religion in general. The material in this unit can equally be approached from a linguistic, historic or scientific standpoint.

– Students work in groups to answer questions 1 – 3. Answer questions 4 and 5 as a class. If you have a multi-lingual group, question 4 should develop into a fascinating discussion.

Answers

1 *Clockwise from top right:*
   Islam, Hinduism, Buddhism, Ethnic religion (American Red Indian), Christianity
   Centre: Judaism
2 a. *Christianity has approximately 1,783 million followers, and is the largest religion (more than 1/3 of the world)*
   b. *Islam, with approximately 950 million adherents. (Buddhism has approximately 300 million followers, and Hinduism about 700 million.)*
   c. *Hinduism*
   d. *Hinduism*
   e. *Buddhism*
   f. *Christianity*
   g. *Islam*
   h. *Hinduism*
   i. *Islam*
   j. *Christianity*
   k. *All of them, probably*

3 a. *True*

   b. *False. The Koran was written after the death of Muhammad in 632.* (The oldest surviving religious literature is the Vedas, which were begun in about 1,000 BC, and are the scriptures of Hinduism.)

   c. *True*

   d. *False. It was in approximately 1,300 years before Christ.*

   e. *True*

   f. *True.* (The Mormon church was founded by an American, Joseph Smith, in 1830.)

4 Obviously, there are no set answers to this question.

5 Students might mention the religions of people such as the American Red Indians, the Indians of Central and South America, Eskimos or the Australian Aborigines. In Africa there are over 800 ethnic religions.

● Reading (SB 126)

Pre-reading task (SB 126)

– Students will probably not know all of the words in question 1. They can check those they don't know in a dictionary, then read the first part of the article.

– Discuss question 2 as a class. Students might or might not have heard stories about Near Death Experiences, so if they have little to say, move on.

– Students work in pairs to say what they think the order might be of the eight sentences. Stress that it is not important that they get the right answer, but that they think about a possible order and can justify it.

> Three of the sentences mention stages. **Sentence c.** seems to be some sort of introduction to these stages, so that one could come first. **Sentence a.** mentions stage four; **e.** mentions the final stage. **Sentence h.** could come somewhere in between **a.** and **h.** The remaining four sentences discuss the effects of a Near Death Experience. **b.** and **d.** discuss the negative side; **f.** and **g.** possibly describe the positive side.

Reading and matching (SB 126)

– Students read the article and decide which sentence begins which paragraph. Allow adequate time for this, as it is quite a challenging task. Students will probably want to read silently for a few minutes to get an idea of what the article is about, but then encourage them to discuss their answers, and to say why they think a sentence belongs in a certain place.

3 **Answers**

1 *c* (This is an introduction to the stages.)

2 *a* (The article has already mentioned stages 1 and 2. Paragraph 4 describes the third stage, so next is stage four. The next paragraph mentions **a light**. Sentence **a.** refers to the light.)

3 *h* (Sentence **h.** refers to seeing one's whole life again. Paragraph 6 talks about life experiences, and seeing the effects of what one has done during one's life on other people.)

4 *e* (This is the last description of the stages.)

5 *b* (Sentence **b.** is about people not wanting to return to their own bodies. This paragraph quotes an example of someone saying just that.)

6 *d* (The paragraph outlines five negative stages.)

7 *g* (Sentence **g.** refers to people's changed attitudes to death and their belief in an after-life. This paragraph also talks about people losing their fear of death and believing in an afterlife.)

8 *f* (Students might confuse sentences **f.** and **g.** Sentence **g.** must go with 7 for the reason given above. This paragraph mentions some of the spiritual effects of NDE's which sentence **f.** refers to.)

Comprehension check (SB 128)

– Students begin to answer the questions in small groups. Let this go on for five minutes, then ask for feed back. There are a lot of questions in this section, and you will probably want to get a balance between group work and class discussion. The article raises many issues that we think your class will want to discuss.

Answers

1 *There is as yet no objective proof, so we cannot be certain of what experiencers of NDEs describe.*

2 *In stage one, people feel at peace and free from pain. This is both physical and mental, and sounds pleasurable.*
In stage two, people feel detached from their own body, both emotionally and physically, but their mental processes are clear and they can describe events that took place while they were unconscious. Again, it is both physical (feeling weightless) and mental, and whether it sounds pleasurable or frightening depends on the individual.

In stage three, people find themselves moving rapidly down a tunnel towards a light. This is presumably a mental sensation, and again, whether it is pleasurable or frightening depends on the individual.

In stage four, people emerge into the light. There are feelings of love and peace. They see their life again, and see the effects of what they have done on other people. It could be argued that this is both a physical and mental sensation, as movement is involved, but the movement is all in the mind. Some parts sound pleasurable (love, joy, beauty and peace), and some parts sound frightening (feeling the results of all that one has done on other people).

In stage five, people enter the light. They meet dead relatives who usually tell them that they must return to earth. The answer to the other questions is the same as in stage four.

3 The fact that experiencers of NDEs can describe in some detail events that took place while they were supposedly unconscious.

4 We don't really know! Experiencers seem to be able to see into people's minds and know what they are thinking.

5 The prospect of seeing one's whole life in review is frightening enough, but seeing the effects of all that you have done on other people is indeed momentous. The writer suggests that this might illustrate how all people are in fact linked in conscience.

6 Dead relatives or loved ones tell them that their time on earth is not yet up. They have to return because their purpose on earth has not been fulfilled or because they must help their family on earth. It is not a person's physical health or condition which decides whether a person dies.

7 He found it restrained and constricted, without control and robot-like. He called the life he had experienced after death 'truly real life', because it was so much fuller, more complete and peaceful than life on earth.

8 They have a changed attitude to death, and they think it possible that there is an afterlife. They lose their fear of death. They have an enhanced appreciation of things both big and small in life. They become more tolerant. They have an increased sense of self-worth. Spiritual matters are more important than material ones. Many people reassess their religious beliefs, not adhering themselves to any one religion, but feeling that there is an essential unity of all faiths.

9 These depend on your point of view. Whatever makes people hate each other is a barrier to communication. It could be religions that urge followers to kill people who believe in other religions. It could be intolerance, racial prejudice or nationalism that drive people away from each other.

10 Glimpses into the future of coming world events. They predict a world of horrific calamity. This is the result of our violating natural and spiritual laws.

11 NDEs aren't just interesting for the people who have experienced them. They tell us all (if they are correct) something about our life and what we can expect after it. They stress the importance of spiritual values. The prospect of such calamities is the crisis; but the possibility of avoiding them by obeying natural and spiritual laws more closely is the opportunity.

What do you think?   (SB 128)

– Discuss the 'What do you think?' questions as a class.

▶ **Language focus**   (SB 131, TB 95)

● Vocabulary 1   (SB 128)

Noun collocations   (SB 128)

– Read the introduction as a class.

Answers
1 a. *bar*
   b. *joint*
   c. *drop*
   d. *stick*
   e. *clove*
   f. *pinch*
   g. *dash*
   h. *clap*
   i. *flash*
   j. *spell*
   k. *gust*
   l. *patch*
   m. *breath*
   n. *round/burst*
   o. *bit*
   p. *speck*
   q. *pane*
   r. *splinter*
   s. *sample*

2 a. *luck/genius/work*
   b. *God/mercy/aggression*
   c. *emergency/repair/health/play/mind*
   d. *golf/drinks/toast/visits/ammunition*
   e. *sand/rice/truth*
   f. *anger/despair/energy/enthusiasm*

3 Students work in pairs to write questions which will elicit the use of some of the above collocations. Don't worry if the dialogues sound somewhat contrived, as this is an accuracy-based activity.

– There is another exercise to practise noun collocations in the Workbook.

● Listening (SB 129)

T.27

Pre-listening task (SB 129)

– Discuss the questions in the pre-listening task as a class. Some are quite difficult, not in the language required, but in their philosophical scope and the scientific knowledge required.

Answers

There are no set answers to question 1.

2 *The Christian Old Testament says that God made the world in six days. First He created light, then divided the earth and the water, then made day and night, then created all the living creatures, and finally made man and woman in his own likeness.*

According to Hindus, this is not the first world or universe. There have been and will be many more. Universes are made by Brahma, the Creator, maintained by Vishnu, the preserver, and destroyed by Shiva. From the destruction comes new life.

The Muslim religion says that God created the world and the heavens, and all the creatures on the face of the earth. He ordered angels to go to the earth and bring a handful of soil, which He moulded into a model of a man. He breathed life and power into it, and immediately it sprang to life. This was the first man, Adam.

Darwin's theory of evolution proposed that man had descended from apes, and was not, therefore, the direct creation of God.

3 *Cosmologists believe that the universe is expanding, and therefore galaxies used to be much closer together. Between ten and twenty thousand million years ago, there was a huge explosion, known as the big bang, which shot matter throughout the universe.*

Haldane's comment suggests not only that our understanding is incomplete, but that human beings do not have the capacity to understand the truth, whatever that might be.

– Students answer question 4 on their own, looking up any words they don't know. You could relate the opening words of the interview to the photographs showing the place of the Earth in the Solar System and the Milky Way.

– Students continue to look up words they don't know in question 5.

Listening for information (SB 129)

– Students listen to the interview and answer the questions.

Answers

1 *Because they want to believe that there is something special and central about human beings, while Darwin says that man is just another animal.*
2 *The fact that man is deeply connected with all other living things on Earth.*
3 *Scientists can see what is happening now to the universe, and most evidence suggests that it is expanding. This expansion must have been going on for millions and millions of years. Looking back into the past is like running a film backwards. It tells us that the universe probably did begin with the big bang.*
4 *The key question is whether the big bang as we understand it was the first of its kind, or whether the universe is bound in an endless cycle of expansion and contraction.*
5 *In the beginning God created the heaven and the earth. And the earth was without form, and void; and darkness was upon the face of the deep. (Genesis)*

▶ **Language focus** (SB 131, TB 95–6)

● Vocabulary 2 (SB 130)

T.28

Synonyms and their associations (SB 130)

– Read the introduction as a class. Students read through the *Desiderata*, and answer the question about how it avoids expressing the views of any one religion.

Answer

It offers commonsensical advice about how to cope with life and other people. It urges people to be at peace with God, whatever they conceive Him to be.

– Students read the *Desiderata* again, deciding which of the three words best fills each gap. Point out that sometimes there is a semantic reason why a word doesn't fit, and at other times it is to do with style.

Answers

a. **clearly** (**Articulately** *is not the point.* **Unambiguously** *sounds very cumbersome in such a simple text.*)
b. **dull** (**Dim** *is colloquial and means stupid. The idea that one should listen to* **gloomy** *i.e.* **miserable** *people doesn't fit the message.*)
c. **aggressive** (**Touchy** *is too informal.* **Argumentative** *could fit.*)
d. **bitter** (**Twisted** *would also fit the idea. You are* **bitter** *about yourself, which is the message here, but you are* **spiteful** *towards other people.*)
e. **humble** (**Trivial** *and* **insignificant** *are too negative and dismissive.*)

f. **fortunes** (**Hazards** *suggest that danger is everywhere. We cannot talk about* **opportunities** *of time – the words don't collocate.*)

g. **trickery** (**Intrigue** *could also fit.* **Strategies** *are neither positive or negative, while what is needed here is a negative quality. Also, the meaning is wrong, and doesn't fit here.*)

h. **strive** (**Struggle** *is too negative. The preposition with* **strive** *is* **for**, *but* **endeavour** *is usually followed by an infinitive.*)

i. **feign** (**Feign** *is the only word that applies to emotions. You* **fake** *or* **forge** *pictures or bank notes.*)

j. **gracefully** (**Willingly** *sounds too strong.* **Elegantly** *makes the action sound too vain.*)

k. **shield** (**Protect** *and* **guard** *would also fit.*)

l. **loneliness** (**Loneliness** *expresses how one feels about being alone, whereas* **solitude** *tells only the physical state. One can be lonely in a crowd of people – one doesn't have to be isolated to feel lonely.*

m. **right** (**Role** *and* **privilege** *don't fit semantically or grammatically.*)

n. **unfolding** (**Proceeding** *and* **progressing** *are just possible, given that this is a sort of poem. We talk about a story* **unfolding**, *but none of the three words commonly collocate with universe.*)

o. **sham** (**Pretence** *would also fit.* **Swindle** *is too colloquial, and is countable. What is needed here is an uncountable noun.*)

– Students listen to the recording to check their answers. Talk about whether they think any of their words were better, but make sure their suggestions fit both semantically and grammatically.

Although there are certain archaic words such as **amid**, the overall feel of the text is modern. Much of it sounds like 1960 hippy talk (*You are a child of the universe; it is . . . a beautiful world*) and there are many modern turns of phrase (*they too have their story; enjoy your achievements; keep interested in your own career*).

LANGUAGE STUDY (SB 131)

1 Nouns with a special meaning in the plural (SB 131)

– Read the introduction as a class.

Practice (SB 131)

– Students will probably need to look up most of the words in their dictionary. You could give half of the class words a – g, and the other half words h – m.

When they have finished, they explain their words to the other group.

Sample Answers

a. *An orange is a kind of fruit.*
   After years of hard work, he is finally reaping the fruits of his labour.

b. *Sight is one of the five senses.*
   I want to see the sights of London.

c. *I've got a pain in my arm.*
   He took great pains to hide his disappointment at not being offered the job.

d. *It has been an honour to work with you.*
   I have an honours degree in French.

e. *Charity begins at home.*
   There are thousands of charities in this country.

f. *It is a custom to take fruit to someone in hospital.*
   When going through Customs, you must declare any imported goods.

g. *The plane landed smoothly on the ground.*
   She was granted a divorce on grounds of adultery.

h. *I enjoy my work.*
   A brick works (= factory), or the works of William Shakespeare.

i. *Some people believe our spirit lives on after death.*
   He's been in low spirits for the past few weeks.

j. *We get oxygen through the air we breathe.*
   She puts on terrible airs and graces. I don't know who she thinks she is.

k. *He has a very warm manner with people.*
   It's bad manners to talk with your mouth full.

l. *The storm caused a lot of damage.*
   He was awarded ten thousand pounds' damages in the court case.

m. *Surgery was necessary to remove the bullet.*
   Doctors' surgeries are busy places.

– There is an exercise to practise nouns in the singular and plural in the Workbook.

---

2 'They' referring to a singular person (SB 131)

– Read the introduction as a class.

Practice (SB 131)

Answers

a. them . . . their . . . them
b. they
c. they
d. their
e. their
f. themselves
g. their
h. they
i. they . . . their

3 The use of '-ever' for emphasis (SB 131)

– Read the introduction as a class.

Practice (SB 132)

Answers

a. *Whoever*
b. *whoever . . . whatever*
c. *wherever*
d. *However*
e. *Whenever . . . whatever*
f. *whatever*
g. *However*
h. *wherever*
i. *whoever*
j. *Wherever . . . however*

4 The use of '-ever' to express surprise (SB 131)

– Read the introduction as a class. Ask students to practise the sentences, paying attention to sentence stress and intonation – they must sound surprised!

Practice (SB 132)

– Students work in pairs to think of some appropriate questions.

Answers

a. *What on earth are they going there for?*
However are they going to manage to fit into one caravan?
Whatever are they going to do in Siberia?

b. *What on earth did he do that for?*
Whatever is he going to do with it?

c. *Whatever are we going to give them to eat?*
Wherever can they sleep?
Why on earth did they come here at this time?

d. *What on earth does he think he's doing?*
Whatever did he give up his job for?
How on earth is the family supposed to live?

e. *Whatever does his wife think?*
What ever does he want with a python?
Where on earth is he going to keep it?

REVISION (SB 132)

Review of input (SB 132)

– This exercise could be done as homework and then checked in groups in class.

Answers

Dear Anna
Thanks for your letter. Naturally, I was sorry to hear about your aunt's fall. I hope she'll feel better soon. She must be getting on now – how old is she exactly? It must have been horrible for her to fall and not be able to get someone to help her. If she didn't live on her own, people wouldn't be so worried, but old people are so stubborn and want their independence. Give her my regards when you next see her, and tell her I think she's very brave.

You have classes every week at nightschool, don't you? You say you have four three-hour exams next week. Good luck with them. You can only do your best – you can't do more than that. You say you're working hard – I'm most impressed! You never used to work for your exams. You said you didn't have to, because you always found exams so easy. Anyway, try to do your best this time!

Since I last wrote to you, I've had an accident. Nothing serious. I went to a very strange party given by Alan, who I told you about in my last letter. At first I didn't want to go, because I was feeling tired, but in the end I changed my mind and went. Alan introduced me to his girlfriend, who I had never met before. She was absolutely delightful, but the others were all rather odd, and I couldn't think of anything to talk to them about. If Alan weren't a close friend, I wouldn't have gone to the party. Anyway, what happened is that I tripped over a table and knocked myself out! I don't know how it happened. I couldn't have had too much to drink because I had only just arrived when it happened. I was taken to hospital for an X-ray, because they were worried in case I had broken my arm, which was swollen. When I came round, I was lying on a hospital bed. I felt fine after a few hours' rest and went home. I sent Alan a bunch of flowers to apologize for the trouble I had caused – did I do right? (or did I do rightly) What would you have done in my situation? Would you have done the same as I did?

It's time you came to see me. Spring is coming, and the flowers should be out soon. If you want me to find out about train times, I'll do it for you.

Keep in touch. Write soon.

Best wishes,

Serge

EXTRA IDEAS

– You could interview English-speaking friends on the subject of religion in their lives, perhaps comparing the place of religion now to one or two generations ago.

– Students could report on varying attitudes to religion amongst the generations of their family and friends.

– If you have a multi-lingual class, it can be fascinating to hear about different religious beliefs and practices.

– Use the supplementary reading text on page 97 of this Teacher's Book, about a man who, under hypnosis, was taken back through his childhood to the day he was born.

PRIMAL screams apart, not many people can remember their birth and early days of infancy. Fewer still, primal screamers included, can go even further back to life in the womb. Playwright Bill Morrison appeared to manage this feat, aided by a (bona fide) hypnotist, a producer, and a tape-recorder, in a BBC radio programme called Spring of Memory earlier this year. In the programme, the outcome of 12 sessions held over several weeks, Bill appears to regress under hypnosis, beginning when he is a schoolboy living near Belfast during the war and ending at a few months after conception.

Memory under hypnosis is notoriously unreliable. Leonard Wilder, the hypnotist who worked with Bill, is quick to say that out of 20 subjects you might get 10 "with errors". But there are certain tests and memory checks. A hypnotist will ask subjects before hypnosis for their telephone number when they were children, and their address at the age of 7 and the colour of the bicycle they were given for a fifth birthday.

"If they say they do not remember I ask again when they are under hypnosis and may get the number and address, and the colour of the bicycle and the chip on the left-hand side." Sometimes when a taped recording of the session is played back, subjects will say they do remember now, and the details they gave are correct. Others will go home and verify. Presumably 10 out of 20 have got it right.

It doesn't necessarily follow that they'd get birth memories right too, but Bill Morrison's hypnosis produced authentic sounds of human anguish and human amazement which came as a total surprise to him (he says). On the tape we hear Bill around the age of 7 deeply upset over the bombing of Hiroshima. At 4 he cries at the thought of war and dying. At 38 Bill says the strength of his emotions came as a shock. He'd thought the war had hardly touched him and only after hypnosis can remember the tension of listening to the six o'clock news, the fear that the enemy was perhaps only round the corner and the need to listen to the way adults talk so that he would be able to survive on his own if necessary.

At two he complains. "I've got nothing to do," and at the request of the hypnotist displays some uneven knowledge of the alphabet ... "A – B – D – E – G ..." As Bill gets younger his language becomes more primitive and hesitant, and he is given

Bill Morrison was taken under hypnosis back to the day he was born. And a frightening old world it turned out to be, he recalls. Helen Franks reports.

I wanna hold your hand

"permission" by the hypnotist to use words.

Looking back on the sessions with the hypnotist, he recalls: "There was a struggle between my adult self that would use explicit expressions and the self that would use the word I knew at the age, say, of two and a half." The struggle got stronger and stronger but somehow I couldn't be untrue to the stage of development.

At three months there are inconsequential burblings, the humming of some lullaby that Bill is not able to identify out of hypnosis though he associates it with his mother. He wants to grip with his fingers, and he wants to suck. At two weeks he cries with anger, "No one is coming. Wanna hold. It's not enough. They don't hold me. Something's wrong, they hold me and I move away. The smell is wrong, they don't smell right. So I cry." At four or five hours old he speaks urgently, intently, "I need to eat so much. Eat, eat, eat, eat, eat."

We get to the birth itself. "I'm being pushed. The rhythm's getting stronger. I'm being moved from where I always have been. Quicker and quicker. The strain on my neck is really strong."

There follows a great deal of panting and heavy breathing, a few yelps and gasps. He feels stretched, his body getting longer. There is enormous effort and strain. He seems to be stuck, then pushes again, "I'm so determined."

At a time that seems to be just after the birth, the voice becomes suddenly and unexpectedly quiet. "I've been taken away from where I always have been. I'm too tired to cry but I'm very very sad – so sad. I'm on my own in the light." And then comes the reason for the sadness "I wanted to come out, but I was pushed out."

Whilst saying this, Bill according to his collaborators and his own recall, adopted the foetal position, hands and feet clenched and inward turning. As he regressed further, his features flattened out, his mouth puckered, his speech became slow and slurred.

Now he is a foetus, sometimes moving or pushing, sometimes still. He says he can hear his own heartbeat, and reproduces the sound.

"Tumme . . . tumme . . . tumme . . ."

"Anything else?" urges Leonard.

"Nothing at all . . . tumme . . . tumme . . . tumme" endlessly.

For Bill his own heartbeat is his earliest memory, or his earliest reconstruction.

Bill in his present self says, "Of course it's the adult. It would be impossible for your 38-year-old self to be taken back to an absolutely pure condition. All we were doing was opening keys of memory. A key experience from the past shoots out quite spontaneously under hypnosis." Before the experience he could remember no further back than around the age of seven. Now he feels he has been helped.

"I understand my own history better, in particular my early relationship with my own parents. And all that screaming when I was separated from my mother! I was in real pain. At first I thought, God, I'm really distressed here, and then I thought no I'm not, I'm angry. The other bit of me, the adult bit which knows that I am lying on this couch screaming my head off, began to laugh. That was tremendous, being able to laugh at my own anger. The perspective is so different.

"Another thing that's happened is that I've got rid of pains in my neck and shoulder – they've been troubling me more and more for many years. I discovered that the pains were at the place I seemed to get stuck when I was being born, and since then they've never returned."

What was the biggest revelation? "The strength of the baby – me of course – and the will to be born. The birth was a great moment of liberation, a freedom, a release. There's space, such space. I found the light amazing. It's fine when you are held, but once you are put down you have no understanding of where you are and it seems you have been placed in an endless desert. Survival meant you had to stay awake, so though I was tired I kept awake."

Bill feels very strongly about the importance of touch, of holding the baby.

It sounds, on the basis of this one-man trip, as though Leboyer has got it right. His ideas to ease the trauma of birth and separation include maintaining body contact between mother and baby, as well as regular gentle massage of the baby in the ensuing months. But he also advocates subdued lighting which doesn't at all go with Bill's exhilaration at seeing the light.

Psychoanalysts should be relieved to have their idea of the rage and impotence of the new baby confirmed. But the sense of autonomy is surely a surprise? "I'm so determined" . . . "I wanted to come out" . . . "I need to eat." Not quite such a helpless infant, and perhaps a hint that babies partly fight their own way into the world as well as being pushed.

And where is the primal scream? Bill doesn't seem to have had one. "I was two weeks old when I was separated from my mother in the nursery, and I cried with anger because the smell of the nurses was wrong. But I don't think you could call that a primal scream."

For Bill, the whole enterprise was, he says, therapeutic, not least because he was able to experience his intensities and laugh at them at the same time. But perhaps the most useful insight – especially for parents anxiously seeking solutions to their babies' tears in the pages of Spock or Penelope Leach – is that babies cry because they feel. They may feel lonely, rejected, frightened, hungry, angry. When they don't cry they may feel exhilaration, amazement, curiosity – or just full of milk. Babies, in fact, are human. It's something we tend to forget.

Tuesday December 4 1979

HEADWAY

John & Liz Soars

ADVANCED

TEST BOOKLET

Note to the teacher

There are three tests in this booklet.

Progress Test One covers the work done in Units 1–4.
Progress Test Two covers the work done in Units 5–8.
Progress Test Three covers the work done in Units 9–12.

Each test carries with it a total possible score of 100 marks.

These tests may be photocopied freely for classroom use.
They may not be adapted, printed, or sold without the
permission of Oxford University Press.

Oxford University Press
Walton Street, Oxford OX2 6DP

© Oxford University Press 1989
Typeset by VAP Publishing Services
Printed in Great Britain

Acknowledgements

The publishers and authors would like to thank the following for their
kind permission to use articles, extracts, or adaptations from
copyright material:

The *Evening Standard*: 'Clare puts her heart into Africa' by Lois
Rogers from the issue of 7 March 1989.

Illustrations by RDH Artists

UNITS 1-4

Progress Test One

Exercise 1   Tenses, verb forms and gap fill

In the following newspaper article there are a number of gaps. After some gaps there is a verb in brackets.
Put the verb in the correct tense or verb form (including infinitive, present and past participle).

Example
Yesterday I __went__ (go) to the park.
When there is no verb in brackets, put in one suitable word
– perhaps a noun, an article, a reflexive pronoun, a modal
verb, etc.

Example
The sun rises in __the__ east.

Clare puts her heart into Africa

Clare Mogridge: Setting off tomorrow to join the 'Mother Theresa of Zambia'.

Nurse Clare Mogridge (a) _____ (leave) London to-morrow for a remote part of the African bush (b) _____ (fulfil) the ambition of a lifetime.

Her 45- (c)_____ journey will take her to the isolated settlement of Kabulemema in Zambia, where an elderly British woman (d)_____ (rescue) orphaned babies since 1946.

Clare first heard about the mission at a Sunday school lesson when she was eight, and began writing to its founder, Lilias Falconer.

Determined eventually to join her, Clare qualified (e) _____ a staff nurse and read everything she (f) _____

about African diseases — and finally persuaded 75-(g) _____ -old Miss Falconer to let her (h)_____ (join) her.

Miss Falconer, originally from Chadwell Heath, went to Zambia to work with lepers, but was shocked by the number of babies (i) _____ (leave) to starve after their mothers (j)_____ (die) in childbirth. She began looking after them, and now runs an orphanage (k) _____ (cater) for fifteen children. She also founded a leper settlement and a health centre.

This Mother Theresa of Zambia, who has (l)_____ MA in politics and philosophy, even introduced cows to the region for the first time, and began her own farm and school in the village.

Clare, 23, from Paignton, Devon, said: 'She did her best to put me off going. She said it was rough and primitive, and obviously she was worried about having someone who (m) _____ just become a burden. 'It has taken me years to persuade her I'm serious about it. She began trying (n)_____ (get) me a visa last August.

'That meant a 900- (o)_____ round trip to the nearest town to pick up the form, another 900 miles when it (p)_____ (fill) in, and loads of other trips to hurry the Zambian officials up.'

Clare will have to take anti-malaria pills every day, and give (q) _____ hepatitis injections. She will have to get (r) _____ to a staple diet of 'mush', a flour and water paste with dried meat. Although most of the children grow to adulthood, keeping them away from the crocodile-infested river — the home's only water (s) _____ – is a problem. 'Apparently some people do get eaten by crocodiles,' said Clare.

'Other people have gone out with the intention of helping Miss Falconer and come back again. She relies on one of her first orphans, who's now grown up and married. He does a lot of the work. But she is not (t) _____ strong as she was, and she does now need more help.'

Surrounded by piles of soap, medical textbooks and T-shirts, in the winter sun of Paignton, Clare admitted: 'It's impossible to imagine what it will be like there.'

Total 20

1

Exercise 2   Avoiding repetition

Fill each gap in the following sentences with an auxiliary verb or a modal verb. Sometimes you will need to add **not**.

a. I hope our guests come soon. If they _____, the meal will be spoilt.

b. I thought I'd seen the film before but I _____, so I quite enjoyed it.

c. **A** We're thinking of going to see the photography exhibition.

  B You _____. You'll really enjoy it.

d. **A** Do you think Joanna will have paid off all her debts yet?

  B She _____ _____, but I doubt it. You know what she's like with money.

e. **A** I drove past your house last night, about nine o'clock. I was thinking of popping in.

  B You _____ _____. I wasn't doing anything.

f. I couldn't get my car started this morning. I asked lots

  of people to help, but nobody _____. Isn't that awful?

g. **A** I tried to phone you last night, but you must have been out.

  B I _____. I stayed in all night.

h. I hope you get the job. If you _____, just think how much money you'll earn!

i. **A** I'm thinking of investing all my money in a record shop.

  B I _____. It sounds very risky to me.

j. My children made their own breakfast this morning,

  but I wish they _____. They made a terrible mess.

Total 10

Exercise 3   The future in the past

Put the verb in brackets in an appropriate form of the future in the past.

a. Look at this picture! Do you like it? My father

  _____ (throw) it out, but I told him not to. It really is quite valuable.

b. I left the office and hurried home. I knew there

  _____ (be) a hot meal waiting for me. The very thought of this warmed me up inside.

c. She set the alarm for 7 a.m. The taxi

  _____ (come) at 8.15 to take her to the airport, and she didn't want to be late.

d. **A** What are you doing tonight?

  B I _____ (see) a film with Jack, but he's just rung to call it off.

  A Why don't we go out for a drink, then?

e. **A** Hello. 64778.

  B Hello, Paul. This is Sheila.

  A Hi! I hoped it _____ (be) you. How are you?

Total 5

Exercise 4   Would

In each of the following sentences there is an example of **would**. Write the number 1 if **would** refers to past habit, and 2 if it refers to the future in the past.

a. Every night when I was a child, one of my parents would read me a story, then the other would hold my hands until I fell asleep.

b. I come from quite a poor background. If my parents ever had any money, which was rare, they would pay off their debts and try to clothe us kids.

c. The couple looked round their new house, excited yet anxious. It would be a long time before everything was as they wanted.

d. When I was younger, I would stay up night after night going to parties, but I find I need my sleep these days.

e. Before stepping into the plane, she looked around wistfully at the country she had grown to love. She wanted to savour every last sensation. It would be a long time before she came back.

  a ___ b ___ c ___ d ___ e ___

Total 5

Exercise 5   Verb forms

Write out the Past Simple and the Past Participle of the following verbs.

	Past Simple	Past Participle
a. swear	_____	_____
b. bleed	_____	_____
c. shrink	_____	_____
d. swell	_____	_____
e. lay	_____	_____

Total 5

Exercise 6   A or an?

Put **a** or **an** before the following words.

a. ___ uniform

b. ___ honest face.

c. ___ EEC policy

d. ___ UN fact-finding mission

e. ___ A-level in maths

Total 5

Exercise 7   As or like?

Put **as** or **like** into each of the following gaps.

a. _____ his father before him, James emigrated at the age of eighteen in search of adventure.

b. He also got married at the age of twenty, just _____ his father had done.

c. Using his front room _____ an office, he opened up an export/import business.

d. Listen to that music! It sounds _____ a circus!

e. She is regarded _____ one of our greatest living poets.

Total 5

Exercise 8   Modal verbs, present and past

Fill the gap in the second sentence by putting the concept expressed by the verb form in the first sentence into the past. In some cases a different form of the modal verb is needed, and in others a totally different verb.

a. She *must be working* late. She isn't at home.

   She _____ late. She looked very tired when I saw her.

b. I *can come* next week, if you like.

   I _____ last week. What a pity we didn't think of it.

c. I *can escape* if I can reach that window.

   I _____ by climbing through a window. Then I jumped down and ran away.

d. I'll answer the phone. *It'll be* for me.
   Was the man you met quite tall with grey hair and a

   beard? That _____ my father!

e. You *needn't worry*. We'll be perfectly safe.

   You _____ about me. I was perfectly safe the whole time.

Total 5

Exercise 9   Modal verbs, positive and negative

Fill the gap in the second sentence by putting the concept expressed by the verb form in the first sentence into the negative.

a. The painting *must have been stolen*.

   The painting _____! It's too big to get out of the room.

b. If the traffic isn't too bad, he *could be* here by 3.00.

   He _____ here until 5.00 if he gets stuck in a jam.

c. You *must work* hard!

   You _____ so hard! You're a millionaire!

d. You *must work* hard!

   You _____ so hard! Can't you see you're killing yourself?

e. I *need to see* a doctor.

   You _____ doctor. A chemist can prescribe something for you.

Total 5

Exercise 10   Transformation

Finish each of the following sentences in such a way that it means exactly the same as the sentence printed before it.

a. Provided you tell me where you are, I don't mind where you go.

   As _____

b. I think you should tell the truth.

   You had _____

c. I am always thinking about the accident.

   I can't _____

d. We wanted to put out the fire.

   We tried _____

e. Why don't you ask John to help you?

   Try _____

f. I earn £500. David earns £1,000.

   David earns twice _____

g. They made me resit the exam.

   I was _____

h. Nearly five hundred people are believed to have drowned.
   As _____

i. I thought I would do worse in the exam.

   I didn't _____

j. Don't touch these papers.

   I don't want _____

Total 10

Exercise 11   Homophones

The following sentences contain two homophones written in phonemic script. Write out the correct spelling of the homophones.

Example   *Can you /siː/ the /siː/?*
            see   sea

3

a. There's a squirrel in my garden. It /berɪz/ /berɪz/ everywhere.

_____ _____

b. He took his /sɔ:d/ and /sɔ:d/ a hole in the wood.

_____ _____

c. There are some people on my language /kɔ:s/ who tell /kɔ:s/ jokes.

_____ _____

d. She was /kɔ:t/ speeding and had to go to /kɔ:t/.

_____ _____

e. When she /preɪz/, she gives /preɪz/ to God.

_____ _____

Total 10

Exercise 12   Vocabulary

Fill the gaps with words that appeared in Units 1–4 of Headway Advanced. Each dash (_) represents one letter. The first letter of each word is provided as a clue.

a. You are this if you don't like the sight of blood!

s _ _ _ _ _ _ _

b. If you get mud on your shoes, you need a knife to

s _ _ _ _ _ the mud off!

c. This verb describes how you sit in a chair if you feel

tired or bored. s _ _ _ _ _

d. A word, meaning gifted, to describe an artist.

t _ _ _ _ _ _ _

e. Another word for *strategies*.

t _ _ _ _ _ _

f. A word which means *a new and successful development or achievement*.
For example, scientists have made a

b _ _ _ _ _ _ _ _ _ _ in their search for a cure
for cancer.

g. We talk about an *enemy* in a war, but what about in love or in business?

r _ _ _ _

h. If you do this to someone, you tell them a lie.

d _ _ _ _ _ _

i. If you can't bear the level of noise, you find it

i _ _ _ _ _ _ _ _ _ _.

j. Your clothes are this if you've been wearing them all day, or if they haven't been neatly folded.

c _ _ _ _ _ _

k. Another word for *very ugly*.

h _ _ _ _ _ _

l. If you are in a lot of pain, you are in

a _ _ _ _ .

m. A verb which means *to tremble with fear, horror or disgust.*

s _ _ _ _ _ _

n. A word which means *strange*, for example an owl hooting in the middle of the night.

e _ _ _ _

o. Another word for *pleased* or *grateful* for what someone has done for you.

a _ _ _ _ _ _ _ _ _ _ _

Total 15

Score

Exercise 1	_____	out of 20
Exercise 2	_____	out of 10
Exercise 3	_____	out of 5
Exercise 4	_____	out of 5
Exercise 5	_____	out of 5
Exercise 6	_____	out of 5
Exercise 7	_____	out of 5
Exercise 8	_____	out of 5
Exercise 9	_____	out of 5
Exercise 10	_____	out of 10
Exercise 11	_____	out of 10
Exercise 12	_____	out of 15

Total   _____

          100

Percentage
Total ☐ / %

Progress Test Two

Exercise 1   Tenses, verb forms and gap fill

In the following article there are a number of gaps. After some gaps there is a verb in brackets.
Put the verb in the correct tense or verb form, active or passive.

Example
Yesterday I __went__ (go) to the park.
When there is no verb in brackets, put in one suitable word.
This could be a preposition, an adverb, a modal verb etc.

Example
The sun sets __in__ the west.

Criminals to apologize face to face

Criminals could (a) _____ (make) to meet their victims face to face in order to apologize (b) _____ their crimes, under a new approach to punishment now (c) _____ (plan) by the Home Office.

(d) _____ government ministers are also discussing is the idea that offenders (e) _____ repair any damage they (f) _____ (cause) to property, and return personally any stolen goods.

"(g) _____ , the finer points of the scheme need more careful working out," said Mr Leon Brittan, the Home Secretary, "but the government wants to signal an important shift in its thinking away from offenders towards victims."

Next Wednesday, when Mr Brittan (h) _____ (address) an audience of London lawyers, he (i)_____ (unveil) this new emphasis on personal reparation and compensation by criminals to their victims.

Ministers believe that public confidence in the criminal justice system (j) _____ (boost) by this new focus on victim support. They are convinced (k)_____ the value of making offenders confront the suffering directly caused by their crimes. They argue (l)_____ that many criminals (m)_____ think twice about (n)_____ further crimes once they (o)_____ (face) with the misery and hardship of their victims.

"Several parts of the country (p) _____ already_____ (experiment) with such schemes," said Mr Brittan. "By next year we believe the number (q)_____ (multiply) tenfold. In Merseyside a young man who (r)_____ previously _____ (serve) many (s)_____ for burglary, gave up criminal activity completely after he (t)_____ (force) to return to his victim's house and mend all the broken windows. He has even become a close friend of his victim!"

Total 20

Exercise 2

Finish each of the following sentences in such a way that it means the same as the sentence printed before it.

a. I don't like the long, dark nights of winter.

What _____

b. I admire Cathy. She always dresses so tastefully.

What I admire _____

c. You should go to Marks and Spencer, they have the best quality underwear.

Marks and Spencer is _____

d. The talks about arms reduction seem to be making progress. This pleases me greatly.

What_____

e. 'Well done! You've decorated this room beautifully.' Sandra said to Tanya.

Sandra complimented Tanya _____

f. Eliza worked hard at her vowel sounds and now she can say them beautifully.

If Eliza _____

g. I can't pick it up for you tomorrow. I'm not going into town.

If I _____

h. They accused him of starting the riot.

He was blamed _____

i. I'll kill the dragon and I'll rescue the princess!

When _____

j. She researched the subject thoroughly before starting to write the book.

Once she _____

Total 10

Exercise 3   Adverbs and expressions of opinion

Fill each gap in the following conversation with a suitable adverb or expression of opinion. Choose from the list below. Use each adverb or expression only once.

A Have you seen the new production of 'My Fair Lady' at the Theatre Royal?

B Yes I have. (a) _____, it's my favourite musical. I went on the first night, but (b)

_____, I was a bit disappointed in the production.

A Were you? We saw it last night and loved it. (c)

_____ Julia Day had difficulty getting the Cockney accent for Eliza Doolittle,

but (d) _____ she was chosen for the part because of her beautiful singing voice.

B I suppose so – but she sounded more American than Cockney!

(e) _____, guess who I saw in the audience with his new wife!

incidentally   quite honestly   presumably
as a matter of fact   admittedly

Total 5

Exercise 4   Adjective order

Put the adjectives in brackets into an order which sounds natural.

a. How much did you pay for that _____,

_____, _____ plate?
(Wedgwood; patterned; exquisite)

b. You can't wear those _____, _____,

_____, _____ socks for tennis.
(cotton; green; ankle; ghastly)

c. We've bought a _____, _____,

_____, _____ desk.
(antique; mahogany; fabulous; large)

d. It's my _____, _____,

_____ record. (sixties'; favourite; Beatles')

e. I love those _____, _____,

_____, _____ windows.
(glass; inspiring; church; stained)

Total 5

Exercise 5   Adverbs with two forms

Underline the correct form of the adverb in the following short conversation.

A Stay (a) **close/closely**. We could (b) **easy/easily** lose each other in this crowd.

B I didn't expect there to be so many people, and they are (c) **most/mostly** teenagers. I thought her type of song would appeal more (d) **direct/directly** to an older audience.

A Push your way to the front. If we sit (e) **right/rightly** at the edge of the stage we'll see and hear beautifully despite the crowd.

Total 5

Exercise 6   Correcting mistakes

In each of the following short paragraphs there are two grammatical mistakes.
Find them and correct them.

a. Where have you bought this delicious, wholemeal bread? Does it sell at the baker's on the corner?

b. While she was loading the gun, her mouth had formed a horrible, toothless grin. Then she turned and was pointing the gun at us.

c. I had never done my own decorating before, and I really enjoyed doing it, until my family complained over the colour scheme. They have insisted at my repainting the living room white.

d. I've never been to the theatre when I lived in London. It's such a pity because I would have enjoyed it if I did.

e. Don't get me wrongly. Generally I love reading, but every time I start to read this novel I'll immediately fall asleep.

f. You would never believe the number of novels Barbara Cartland has written every year. If only I would find a publisher for my stories.

g. If I knew John was going to be there, I would have returned the book I had borrowed from him last week.

h. You're welcome to stay for supper, but there wouldn't be much to eat. The groceries won't deliver until tomorrow morning.

i. I don't want you to mention this to her until we'll have discussed the problem. Then we are able to offer a solution.

j. **A** How long have you come here for your holidays?
   B This is our third visit and we intend that we return again next year.

Total 20

Exercise 7   Vocabulary – Adverb and verb collocation

Fill each gap with an appropriate adverb.

Example
They discussed the plan very ___thoroughly.___

It was raining (a) _____ as Nigel and Fiona made their way across the sodden fields. Night had fallen,

and they could see the (b) _____-lit windows of the cosy little farmhouses on the distant hills. They

thought (c) _____ of the inhabitants settling down for their evening meal or to watch television. Nigel

sensed her distress. He held her hand (d) _____

and whispered (e) _____ in her ear: 'Be strong, Fiona. Remember I love you. We'll soon be there.'

Total 5

Exercise 8   Vocabulary – a crossword

All the words in the crossword appeared in Units 5–8 of Headway Advanced.
Solve the clues and complete the crossword.

ACROSS

1. The shirt or jumper is too big, but perhaps this is fashionable!

3. This is lowered at a castle so that you can cross the moat.

6. The noise a fire makes when wood is burning.

8. A jacket worn as part of a school uniform or worn perhaps by an umpire at a tennis match.

9. Patterned in lines – like a tiger.

11. This is sleeveless and sometimes part of a man's suit.

12. A rough, unfinished edge of material. F_____ jeans are often popular.

13. A warrior used to carry this in one hand and a sword in the other to protect himself.

16. When the colour is lost usually because of age or the sunlight.

17. An all-in-one garment often worn by babies, but also at one time popular with adults and not always at sporting events.

18. You fight like this if you are brave.

DOWN

1. Prison camps or fields can be painful to get out of if this is part of the fence.

2. This homonym is what cows or sheep do in meadows, and is what children often have on their knees if they fall over.

4. This kind of vest protects you against gunshot.

5. You do this in amazement.

6. You did this eating an apple or your feet did it when walking on a gravel path.

7. This kind of shelter protected a lot of people from bombs in the Second World War.

10. This kind of skirt has a lot of little folds, as in a Scotsman's kilt.

14. This homonym is something you take on a picnic, and is a verb that means impede or prevent – progress for example.

15. This homonym is both what you might do to important documents and what you might do to your finger nails.

Total 20

7

Exercise 9   Pronunciation – odd man out

In the following lists of words, three words rhyme.
Underline the one that is different.

a. creak   steak   squeak   shriek
b. spear   wear   cheer   leer
c. tomb   boom   broom   bomb
d. howl   growl   bowl   prowl
e. shed   said   raid   tread

Total 5

Exercise 10   Pronunciation – word stress

Mark the stress in the following words.

a. dungarees   pin-striped suit
b. preferable   prefer
c. relative   relation
d. influenza   diphtheria
e. barometer   barometrical

Total 5

Score

Exercise 1 _____ out of 20
Exercise 2 _____ out of 10
Exercise 3 _____ out of 5
Exercise 4 _____ out of 5
Exercise 5 _____ out of 5
Exercise 6 _____ out of 20
Exercise 7 _____ out of 5
Exercise 8 _____ out of 20
Exercise 9 _____ out of 5
Exercise 10 _____ out of 5

Total   _____
                    100

Percentage
Total   ⬚ %

UNITS 9-12

Progress Test Three

Exercise 1   Tense usage for fact versus non-fact

Put the verb in brackets in an appropriate tense or verb form.

Wendy Englefield

Don't just sit and worry . . . share your problem with Wendy who's always here to help

My wife and I (a) _____ (have) terrible problems with our teenage daughter. It all began while we were on holiday last year. Kay, my daughter, who is 16, went to a disco and met a man who, she says, she fell passionately in love with. He is 15 years older than her. They (b) _____ (see) each other ever since, and despite all our attempts to dissuade her, she says she wants to marry him.

We have tried to be reasonable parents. It is not just the fact that this man has entered her life that upsets us, although I wish she (c)_____ (never meet) him. If she (d) _____ (not go) to the disco that night, we might still (e)_____ (lead) the life that (f)_____ (make) us so happy until that terrible evening.

She (g) _____ (change) to the point that I hardly recognize her. She stays out all night. I (h)_____ (not mind) if she (i)_____ (tell) us where she is, but she refuses. It is not as though we (j) _____ (be) unreasonable, just protective towards our only child.

She has also left school. I (k)_____ (like) her (l) _____ (stay) on at school until she (m) _____ (be) 18, but she (n) _____ (not listen). She is now working as a cashier in a supermarket, and says that she has no interest in academic subjects. It is a terrible shame. She is naturally bright, and (o)_____ (can) (make) a success of any subject she (p)_____ (turn) her attention to. Before, she wanted to go to university, and I can say without any doubt that she (q)_____ (get) a degree easily. After that, who knows what she might (r)_____ (do)?

Please help us. We are desperate. My daughter behaves as if we (s) _____ (be) strangers. Personally, I feel it is time she (t) _____ (leave) home. What do you think?

John B.
Sheffield

Total 20

9

Exercise 2 Relative clauses

Put in the relative pronouns and the commas that are missing from the following text, which is a reply to the letter in exercise 1. If it is possible to omit the pronoun, add nothing.

Dear Mr B

I was very sorry to hear about the problems

(a) _____ you are having with your daughter

(b) _____ is being most unreasonable, in my opinion. You have tried to see the situation from her point

of view as well as your own (c) _____ is very important if a solution is to be found. Children

(d) _____ parents don't allow them space to develop often rebel, so it is vital that you remain

sympathetic towards the man (e) _____ your daughter has fallen in love with. Patience

(f) _____ we all know is a difficult virtue to practise is your best approach, I feel. Try not to force your

daughter into doing something (g) _____ both you and she might later regret. She doesn't sound like the

most respectful and appreciative child (h) _____ ever was, but you don't want to lose her.

Remember that it is during the teenage years

(i) _____ children do most growing up physically

and emotionally. It is also (j) _____ parents want to throw up their hands in despair and wonder who should leave home, the child or the parents!

Girls (k) _____ usually develop more quickly than boys are often attracted to older men, because they find boys of their own age immature. However, this is a

situation (l) _____ often sorts itself out in later

teens (m) _____ should give you some cause for hope.

Having children is an experience (n) _____

brings great joy, but (o) _____ also involves much responsibility. Don't despair of your daughter! I'm sure things will work out for you.

Total 15

Exercise 3 Nouns in groups

Combine the words in brackets in the following sentences, using one of these patterns.

's (the boy's parents)
of (the) (the Houses of Parliament)
two nouns together (post office)

a. Write your name at the _____ (page; top).

b. Remember to buy some _____ (food; cat) while you're at the shops.

c. Where's the _____ (bowl; cat)? It's time to feed her and I can't find it anywhere.

d. _____ (prices; house) have risen dramatically over the past year.

e. The _____ (living; cost) has also increased.

f. Have you got an empty _____ (box; match)? I want something small to keep some stamps in.

g. The _____ (gunpowder; invention) greatly changed the nature of warfare.

h. _____ (announcement; last week) that the government intends to abolish taxation has left everyone stunned.

i. Did you know that _____ (landlady; Peter) has thirteen children?

j. Have you seen the _____ (exhibition; Spencer; watercolours) yet?

Total 10

Exercise 4 Formal language

In the following letter, underline the item that is more formal.

Dear Ms Baines

(a) | It is with regret that I / I am sorry to | have to (b) | tell / inform | you that

your request for (c) | more / further | credit facilities has been

(d) | rejected. / turned down. | This is (e) | because / due to the fact that | you have

(f) | continued to overdraw / kept on overdrawing | your current account, which is

(g) | at present / now | six hundred pounds overdrawn.

(h) | In my recent letter, / When I last wrote, | you were (i) | requested / asked | to draw

no more cheques on this account, and you (j) | told / assured | me

that you were (k) | making every effort / trying very hard | to restore your account to credit.

(l) | Furthermore, / What is more, | you have continued to use your cash card when you (m) | know / are aware | that you have no funds in your account.

I should be (n) | grateful / happy | if you would (o) | stop / refrain from | using the card and from drawing cheques until the situation has been regularized.

Yours faithfully,

James Lovall

Total 15

Exercise 5   Inversion to express emphasis

Rewrite the following sentences, inverting the subject and the verb, using one of the patterns to express emphasis.

Example

She had never experienced such joy in her life.

Never in her life had she experienced such joy.

a. I have never been so moved by a Shakespeare production.

_____

b. As soon as she closed her eyes, she fell asleep.

_____

c. I only realized how dangerous the situation had been when I got home.

_____

d. Burglars stole a thousand pounds' worth of electrical goods, and left the flat in an awful mess.

_____

e. If we hear any further news, we will be in touch immediately.

_____

f. If it hadn't been for Henry, I might not have met you.

_____

g. He had just started driving his new car when he had an accident.

_____

h. One rarely finds good service these days.

_____

i. She little thought that I knew all about her.

_____

j. She would never again trust her own judgement when buying antiques.

_____

Total 10

Exercise 6   The Present Subjunctive

The verbs in the following sentences are followed either by an **-ing** form or an infinitive. They can all be transformed to be followed by a **that** clause, but some of them will need the Present Subjunctive or **should**. Transform them appropriately.

a. I suggested setting off as soon as possible.

_____

b. The king insisted on his deputy carrying out the order.

_____

c. I propose cancelling the meeting indefinitely.

_____

d. He denied being involved in the robbery.

_____

e. The inquiry recommended fitting smoke hoods into aeroplanes.

_____

Total 5

Exercise 7   Adverb/verb and adverb/adjective collocations

Put an appropriate adverb of intensity (for example, totally, deeply, quite, perfectly, etc.) into each gap. Do NOT use **very** or **really**.

a. I _____ regret not telling the whole truth.

b. I _____ remember writing down the number.

c. But I have _____ forgotten where I wrote it down.

d. As Director, I like to be kept _____ informed of what's going on.

e. She was _____ disappointed when she learned the news.

f. It was _____ obvious that he was dead.

g. I was _____ delighted to hear your news.

h. The solution is _____ simple. I don't know why you can't see it.

i. The room was _____ disgusting. It was dirty, smelly and dark.

j. I was _____ relieved when I finally saw them arriving home.

Total 10

11

Exercise 8 Vocabulary

Fill the gaps and answer the questions with words that appeared in Units 9–12 of Headway Advanced. Each dash (_) represents one letter. The first letter of each word is provided as a clue.

a. What is the opposite of a *serious* crime?
p _ _ _ _

b. A word that means a sudden inspiration, or bright idea.
b _ _ _ _ _ _ _

c. This is what you do to meat or fish if you put it in a sauce before cooking it.
m _ _ _ _ _ _ _

d. Another word for a disadvantage, for example *Your plan is very good, but it has one main _____. It would take too long.*
d _ _ _ _ _ _ _

e. A job is this if it is so simple that you don't need to think about it at all.
m _ _ _ _ _ _

f. A person is this if they are willing to listen to and consider other people's ideas and suggestions.
o _ _ _ - _ _ _ _ _ _

g. A person who is this has the ability to plan things cleverly in order to achieve what they want, often by tricking other people.
c _ _ _ _ _ _

h. Another word for to retreat.
w _ _ _ _ _ _ _

i. A tiny quantity of something, for example, salt.
p _ _ _ _

j. Another word for *period* as in *a _____ of dry weather.*
s _ _ _ _

Total 10

Exercise 9 Vocabulary

Choose the word or phrase which best completes each sentence.

a. He's determined to finish the job
_____ long it takes.
whatever   however   no matter

b. She made a lot of money by _____ paintings by Dutch Masters.
feigning   forging   faking

c. I bought a bottle of expensive perfume from a man in the street, but it turned out to be just coloured water. It was a _____!
swindle   sham   pretence

d. What a horrible day! The sky is dark and
_____ .
dull   gloomy   dim

e. The possibility of a fall is one of the
_____ of rock climbing.
hazards   opportunities   chances

Total 5

Score

Exercise 1	_____	out of 20
Exercise 2	_____	out of 15
Exercise 3	_____	out of 10
Exercise 4	_____	out of 15
Exercise 5	_____	out of 10
Exercise 6	_____	out of 5
Exercise 7	_____	out of 10
Exercise 8	_____	out of 10
Exercise 9	_____	out of 5

Total _____
100

Percentage Total [/ %]

Headway Advanced Tests

Test 1 Units 1–4

Exercise 1

a. is leaving/will leave/will be leaving/leaves
b. to fulfil/ fulfilling
c. hour/day/week
d. has been rescuing/has rescued
e. as
f. could/found
g. year.
h. join
i. left/being left
j. had died/died
k. catering
l. an
m. would/could/might
n. to get
o. mile
p. was/had been filled
q. herself
r. used
s. supply
t. as/so

Exercise 2

a. can't/don't
b. hadn't
c. must/should
d. might/may/ could have
e. should have
f. would/ could/did
g. wasn't
h. do
i. wouldn't
j. hadn't

Exercise 3

a. was going to throw
b. would be
c. was coming
d. was going to see
e. would be

Exercise 4

a. 1
b. 1
c. 2
d. 1
e. 2

Exercise 5

a. swore   sworn
b. bled   bled
c. shrank/shrunk   shrunk/shrunken
d. swelled   swollen/swelled
e. laid   laid

Exercise 6

a. a
b. an
c. an
d. a
e. an

Exercise 7

a. Like
b. as
c. as
d. like
e. as

Exercise 8

a. must have been working
b. could have come
c. managed to escape/was able to escape
d. will have been/would be/would have been
e. needn't have worried

Exercise 9

a. can't/couldn't have been stolen
b. won't be/might not be
c. needn't work/don't need to work/don't have to work
d. mustn't/shouldn't work
e. don't need to see/needn't see/don't have to see

Exercise 10

a. As long as you tell me where you are. I don't mind where you go.
b. You had better tell the truth.
c. I can't help/stop thinking about the accident.
d. We tried to put out the fire.
e. Try asking John to help you.
f. David earns twice as much as I do.
g. I was made to resit the exam.
h. As many as five hundred people are believed to have drowned.
i. I didn't think I would do as/so well in the exam.
j. I don't want anyone/you to touch these papers/these papers to be touched/these papers touched.

Exercise 11

a. buries berries   c. course coarse   e. prays praise

b. sword sawed   d. caught court

Exercise 12

a. squeamish   f. breakthrough   k. hideous

b. scrape   g. rival   l. agony

c. slouch   h. deceive   m. shudder

d. talented   i. intolerable   n. eerie

e. tactics   j. creased   o. appreciative

Tests 2 Units 5–8

Exercise 1

a. be made

b. for

c. being planned/planned

d. What

e. should/will

f. cause/have caused

g. Obviously/Naturally

h. addresses

i. will unveil

j. will be boosted

k. of

l. strongly/forcefully

m. will

n. committing/any

o. are faced/have been faced

p. are already experimenting/ have already been experimenting/ have already experimented

q. will have multiplied

r. had previously served

s. sentences/years

t. was forced/had been forced

Exercise 2

a. What I don't like are the long, dark nights of winter.

b. What I admire about Cathy is the way she dresses so tastefully.

c. Marks and Spencer is where you should go to get e the best quality underwear.

d. What pleases me greatly is the fact that the talks about arms reduction seem to be making progress.

e. Sandra complimented Tanya on the way she had/ 1 how beautifully she had decorated the room.

f. If Eliza hadn't worked hard at her vowel sounds, she wouldn't be able to say them so beautifully.

g. If I were going into town tomorrow, I could (have) pick(ed) it up for you.

h. He was blamed for starting the riot.

i. When I've killed the dragon, I'll rescue the princess!

j. Once she had researched the subject thoroughly, she started writing the book.

Exercise 3

a. As a matter of fact   c. Admittedly   e. Incidentally

b. quite honestly   d. presumably

Exercise 4

a. that exquisite, patterned, Wedgwood plate

b. those ghastly, green, cotton, ankle socks

c. a fabulous, large, antique, mahogany desk

d. my favourite, sixties', Beatles' record

e. Those inspiring, stained-glass, church windows

Exercise 5

a. close   c. mostly   e. right

b. easily   d. directly

Exercise 6

a. did you buy   Is it sold/Do they sell it

b. her mouth formed   pointed/the gun

c. complained about   insisted on

d. I never went   if I had

e. get me wrong   I immediately fall

f. Barbara Cartland writes   I could find

g. I had known   I borrowed

h. there won't be   groceries aren't delivered/won't be delivered

i. until we have discussed   we will be able

j. have you been coming here   we intend to return

Exercise 7

Sample answers

a. heavily/hard/steadily

b. brightly/dimly/well

c. longingly/enviously/wistfully

d. tightly/lovingly

e. softly/passionately/encouragingly/tenderly/lovingly/ reassuringly

Exercise 8

Exercise 9

The following are the words that are different.

a. steak   c. bomb   e. raid

b. wear   d. bowl

Exercise 10

a. dunga′rees ′pin-striped ′suit

b. ′preferable pre′fer

c. ′relative re′lation

d. influ′enza diph′theria

e. ba′rometer baro′metrical

Test 3 Units 9–12

Exercise 1

a. are having/have been having/have
b. have been seeing
c. had never met
d. hadn't gone
e. be leading
f. had made
g. has changed
h. wouldn't mind
i. told/would tell
j. are being/are
k. and l. would like her to have stayed/would have liked her to stay/would have liked her to have stayed
m. was/were
n. wouldn't listen (The Past Simple is not really possible, because it suggests she didn't listen on one occasion only.)
o. could have made/could make
p. turned/had turned
q. would have got/would get
r. have done/do
s. were/are
t. left

Exercise 2

a. (nothing)
b. *daughter*, who
c. *own*, which
d. Children whose parents
e. (nothing)
f. Patience, which we all know is a difficult virtue to practise,
g. (nothing)
h. that/who
i. (nothing)
j. also when parents
k. Girls, who usually develop more quickly than boys,
l. situation that (which is also possible, but two examples of which together is bad style)
m. teens, which
n. experience that
o. but which

Exercise 3

a. the top of the page
b. some cat food
c. the cat's bowl
d. House prices
e. The cost of living
f. matchbox
g. The invention of gunpowder
h. Last week's announcement
i. Peter's landlady
j. the exhibition of Spencer's watercolours

Exercise 4

The following are the more formal items.

It is with regret that I	requested
inform	assured
further	making every effort
rejected	Furthermore
due to the fact that	are aware
continued to overdraw	grateful
at present	refrain from
In my recent letter	

Exercise 5

a. Never have I been so moved by a Shakespeare production.
b. No sooner had she closed her eyes than she fell asleep.
c. Only when I got home did I realize how dangerous the situation had been.
d. Not only did burglars steal a thousand pounds' worth of electrical goods, they also left the flat in an awful mess.
e. Should we hear any further news, we will be in touch immediately.
f. Had it not been for Henry, I might not have met you.
g. Hardly had he started driving his new car when he had an accident/No sooner had he started driving his new car than he had an accident.
h. Rarely does one find good service these days,
i. Little did she think that I knew all about her.
j. Never again would she trust her own judgement when buying antiques.

Exercise 6

a I suggested that we (should) set off as soon as possible.
b. The king insisted that his deputy (should) carry out the order.
c. I propose that the meeting (should) be cancelled indefinitely.
d. He denied that he was/had been involved in the robbery.
e. The inquiry recommended that smoke hoods (should) be fitted in aeroplanes.

Exercise 7

Sample answers

a. deeply/sincerely/bitterly
b. distinctly/clearly
c. totally/completely
d. fully
e. bitterly/terribly/greatly
f. quite/totally/absolutely
g. absolutely/quite
h. perfectly/terribly/quite
i. utterly/absolutely/quite
j. greatly/deeply

Exercise 8

a. petty
b. brainwave
c. marinade
d. drawback
e. mindless
f. open-minded
g. cunning
h. withdraw
i. pinch
j. spell

Exercise 9

a. however
b. faking
c. swindle
d. gloomy
e. hazards